Dew Drop Inn

Lasting memories of a Cookshire landmark

Winston C. Fraser

© 2017 Winston Fraser Consulting Inc.

1225 rue Bellevue
Saint-Lazare, QC J7T 2L9
438-969-2510
wcfraser@sympatico.ca

All rights reserved. No part of this book may be adapted, reproduced or transmitted in any form or by any means, electronic, mechanical, photocopying, recording, microrecording, or otherwise, without the written permission of Winston Fraser Consulting Inc.

Layout and production: Jim Fraser

Front cover: From a painting by Barbara Keys Lassenba

Dedication page photo: Ayer's Cliff School portrait, Fraser family archives

Back cover photos: Fraser family archives

Printed and bound in Canada by:

Katari Imaging
282 Elgin St.
Ottawa, ON K2P 1M3
613-233-1999
www.katariimaging.com

ISBN: 978-0-9950842-2-3

Contents

Dedication 4

Preface 5

Acknowledgements 6

Chapter 1   In the beginning 7

Chapter 2   Room at the inn 21

Chapter 3   Eat, drink and be merry 35

Chapter 4   All kinds of goods 47

Chapter 5   Signs and wonders 61

Chapter 6   In the upper room 73

Chapter 7   Ride in his chariot 81

Chapter 8   From evening till morning 95

Chapter 9   The fruit of her hands 109

Chapter 10   The rumble of wheels 121

Chapter 11   A time for everything 137

Chapter 12   In the last days 159

Epilogue 169

Appendix   It is written 171

Dedication

This book is dedicated to my late dear cousin, Mabel Fraser McVetty, who, throughout her life, was a constant support to her parents, Ken and Susie Fraser at Dew Drop Inn, and whose detailed daily diaries provided invaluable insight for this book.

Preface

This is a book of memories of a unique place and two very special people.

My Uncle Ken and Aunt Susie Fraser were a couple from very humble beginnings whose extraordinary lives touched many. Under the roof of their home in Cookshire, Quebec, known as Dew Drop Inn, together and individually they plied a wide variety of occupations, trades and activities.

They were innkeepers, storekeepers and restaurateurs. On top of that, Ken was simultaneously sign painter, taxi driver and gas station operator. He also was a serious railroad buff, a baseball fanatic and a great storyteller. Susie was a hairdresser, gardener and needle crafter extraordinaire. She also sang in the Church choir and participated in Women's Guild activities.

After hours they found the time to socialize with family, friends and strangers alike. They were never too busy to lend a generous hand to someone in need. This is their story as recounted by some of us whose lives were enriched by having known them.

Acknowledgements

I wish to acknowledge the invaluable assistance of my cousin, Charles W. K. Fraser, and his family, without whose cooperation this book would not have been possible. In addition, I recognize the contributions of so many others who kindly shared their memories and/or photographs. The list is very long and I apologize in advance to anyone who may have been inadvertently omitted. To all of the following I extend my thanks. Your contributions have made this book what it is – a collection of recollections.

Alberta Everett, Alexandra Pope, Almon Pope, Andrea Fraser, Andrew Scott, Barbara Challies, Barbara Keys Lassenba, Ben Hodge, Betty MacRae Wright, Bob Fitzsimmons, Bob Taylor, Bobbie Bowen, Brian Hodge, Charles C. Fraser, Charlie Twyman, Charlotte Taylor, Christopher Standish, David Fraser, (the late) David Mackay, Diane Fraser Keet, Doris Pope, Dorothy Ross, Dorothy Shelton Dionne, Doug and Eileen McGrory, Dr. Emily Hamilton, Elaine Fraser, Eleanor Vogell Twyman, Elizabeth Fraser Harvey, Elizabeth Hurd Richardson, Frasier Bellam, Gloria Frasier Bellam, Greg Fraser, Jane George, Jean Evans, Jean-François Nadeau, Jim Fraser, Jim Shaughnessy, John "Jack" Fraser, John Gill, Johnny Scholes, Joyce Standish, June Fraser Patterson, Karen Fraser Jackson, Kerri Fraser, Kevin Ross, Louise Knox, Malcolm "Mac" Fraser, Malcolm "Mac" and Jeanne MacLeod, Marilyn Fraser Reed, Marilyn Mackenzie Fraser, (the late) Marina Fraser Tracy, Muriel French Fitzsimmons, Muriel Watson, Neil Burns, Noël Landry, Norma Wiley, Pat Stevenson Smith, Pierre Ellyson, Randi Heatherington, René Bolduc, Rev. John and Arlene Thévenot, Rev. Ron West, Rodger Heatherington, Roger Dionne, Stan Parker, Steve Fraser, Theda Jackson Lowry, Tracie Dougherty and Warren Fraser.

I would be remiss not to mention the very helpful genealogical research provided by Sylvie Champagne and the valuable information contained in the daily diaries kept by my late cousin, Mabel Fraser McVetty, and by my late mother, Alice Hood Fraser. These records that have been preserved by their families constitute a veritable encyclopedia of the family's everyday happenings in the mid-1900s. I also want to thank artist James Harvey for the excellent sketches he created to illustrate scenes for which no photos could be found and Greg Beck for his professional photo retouching. Finally, a special word of appreciation to my brother Jim for his expert proofreading, layout and production services.

I have attempted to accurately credit the sources for all photographs and other images contained in this book. In the case of any missing credits, it can be assumed that the source is the Fraser family archives.

Chapter 1   In the beginning

This story begins more than 100 years before the birth of the Dew Drop Inn, when Ken's and Susie's ancestors emigrated from the British Isles. In 1790, Ken's great-grandfather, Donald Fraser, arrived in Quebec from Scotland as a result of the "highland clearances." About 30 years later, Susie's great-grandfather, Bernard McGuire Sr., arrived from Ireland during a time when his country was promoting the colonization of the part of Lower Canada that came to be known as Megantic County.

Above; Fraser ancestral gravestone, Saint-Gilles, Que. (Photo by Jim Fraser)
Right: McGuire ancestral gravestone, Sainte-Agathe, Que. (www.ancestry.com)

Ken's and Susie's respective Scottish and Irish heritages would later play a significant role in their lives at Dew Drop Inn. For example, every July they would attend the annual Orangeman's Picnic that brought together the descendants of Megantic County pioneers. Daughter Mabel's diary entry for 1959 mentions the picnic and indicates that Susie did not attend that year because she was visiting her mother ("Granny") who was ill at the time:

July 11, 1959: Daddy and Charlie went to picnic. Ma & I to Randboro to see Granny. (Mabel Fraser's diary)

For his part, Ken proudly displayed the Scottish Clan Fraser coat-of-arms in the Dew Drop Inn store.

Ken's background

Kenneth Ira Fraser was born in Cookshire, Quebec, on December 3, 1905, the youngest of three children of Charles Ira Fraser and Lilla Joyce. His dad was a farmer who died when Ken was only five years old. Charles, the 10th of 12 children of James Frasier and Abigail Bailey, was born in the original Fraser farmhouse that was said to be the first framed house in Eaton Township.

Fraser ancestral farmhouse, Cookshire, Que., circa 1898 (Fraser family archives)

Charles Ira Fraser gravestone, Cookshire (Photo by author)

In the beginning

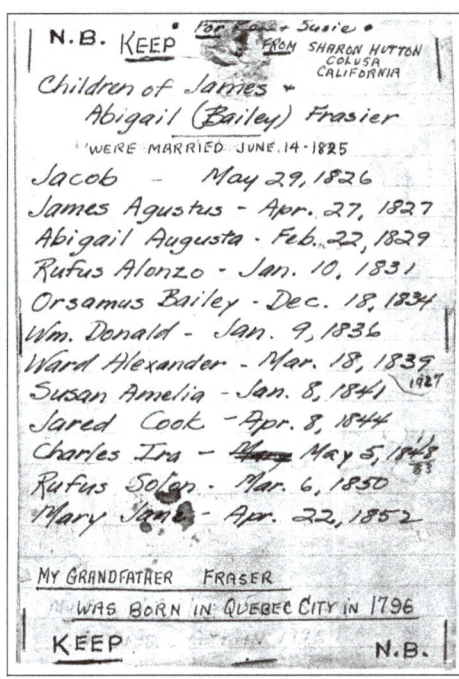

James Frasier and Abigail Bailey's 12 children (Fraser family archives)

Ken's birthplace, Pine Hill Farm in Cookshire (Photo by author)

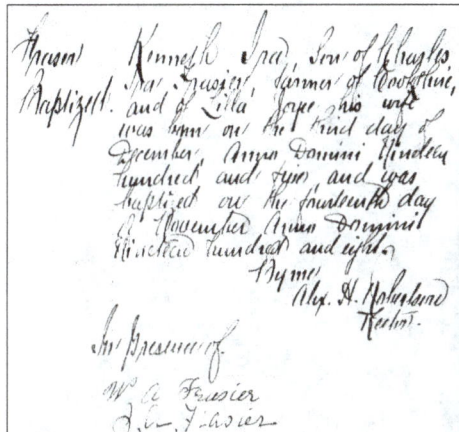

Kenneth Ira Fraser baptismal document, 1908 (www.ancestry.com)

Right: Ken (front) with parents and siblings, circa 1910 (Fraser family archives)

"It doesn't feel cold to me," says young Kenneth (Sketch by James Harvey)

Cookshire Academy, circa 1900 (Postcard from author's collection)

In the beginning

Ken attended elementary and high school at Cookshire Academy, where he won a special prize for history in Grade 5. He worked on the family farm during that time and for a few years afterwards. His older brother Donald (my dad) told me that as a child, Ken was never cold and would often go outside in winter without wearing a coat!

> The following is the prize list of Cookshire Academy for term of 1917:
> Grade XI.—Margaret Kirby, Dorcas Thompson.
> Grade X.—Shirley Macrae, Janet Reid.
> Grade IX.—Homer Lebourveau, N. Warren, Wyatt Johnston.
> Grade VIII.—Mamie Smith, P. Laing. Arithmetic prize, Arthur Ross; History prize, Winnifred Kirby; Progress prize, Hazel Edwards.
> Grade VII.—Louise Charbonnel, Elena French. History prize, Donald Farnsworth; Arithmetic prize, Elena French; English, D. Halls.
> Grade VI.—Rita Butler, Winnifred Drennan. Arithmetic prize, R. Butler; History prize, W. Drennan; Nature Study, Clayton Campbell.
> Grade V.—Kenneth Fraser, Teryl Johnston. History prize, Kenneth Fraser, Graydon Goff; Attendance prize, Lillian Pope, Graydon Goff.

Cookshire Academy prize list, 1917 (Fraser family archives)

Ken (right) with siblings Donald and Maude, circa 1914 (Fraser family archives)

Susie's background

Susan Elizabeth McGuire was born in Lower Ireland, Quebec, on November 5, 1907, the second-youngest of six children of Bernard McGuire and Hannah O'Shea. Her dad was a farmer who died when Susie was only two years old. Susie's mother remarried George Henderson and had four more children by him. The combined McGuire-Henderson family was reflected in the 1921 Canadian census.

Susie attended elementary school in Lower Ireland but had no further formal education. A captioned photograph identifying the school's scholars taken in 1919 does not include Susie, suggesting that at age 11 she was no longer attending school. Her childhood was very difficult. Son Charles describes it this way: "My mother had a tough time as a child. They were poor, extremely poor. The kids went barefoot most of the time – they saved their shoes for the wintertime and

Susan Elizabeth McGuire baptismal document, 1907 (www.ancestry.com)

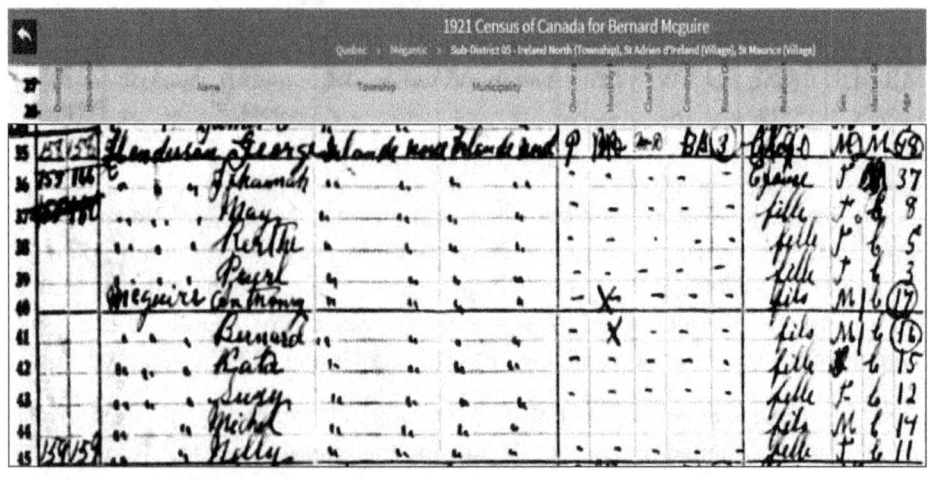

1921 Census of Canada listing for the McGuire-Henderson family (www.ancestry.com)

In the beginning

1919: Lower Ireland School (1840-1944)

Class of 1919: Lower Ireland School
back row (L-R) Will Simons, teacher Jessie Green, Iris Lunnie, Luella Davidson, Garnet and Gladys Thurber
front row (L-R) Harvey Walker, Charlie Robinson, Willie Lunnie, Laura Walker, Evelyn Marshall, Willie Smith, Borden Walker, Guy Davidson, Orlena Davidson

Lower Ireland School and Class of 1919 (Courtesy of Gwen Barry)

things like that." In spite of these hardships, or perhaps because of them, Susie would accomplish much in her adult life.

Susie (far left) and McGuire siblings, 1910 (Courtesy of Johnny Scholes)

When she was 16 years old Susie and her younger sister, Nellie, moved out of the McGuire-Henderson family home in Lower Ireland. Nellie's son, Johnny Scholes, recounts the story:

> The two young girls travelled alone by train to Sawyerville where they knew nobody. The only people that they knew in the surrounding area were some relatives of their stepfather who lived in Island Brook, several miles away. Leaving their trunk at the station, the girls walked all the way to Island Brook to the Henderson's home. Both my mom and Aunt Susie soon got jobs as housekeepers. (Johnny Scholes)

Portrait of Susie, circa 1925 (Courtesy of Johnny Scholes)

In the beginning

Love and marriage

It is very interesting how Ken and Susie came to be a couple. Their son Charles tells the story:

> Mom and Dad first met at the Osgood House hotel in Cookshire. Dad was delivering milk and cream from the farm to the hotel, down at the corner of Main and Railroad streets where the telephone exchange used to be. Mom worked at the hotel as a chambermaid and one of her jobs was to receive the daily dairy delivery. She had previously worked as a chambermaid in Thetford Mines. She later told me that she never minded cleaning toilets as part of her job, but she absolutely hated cleaning spittoons! So that's how they met. Apparently on Dad's first or second visit, Mom was kind enough to offer him a beer. How ironic that was – because, as far as I know, Dad never drank beer in his life! (Charles W.K. Fraser)

Milkman Ken meets chambermaid Susie (Sketch by James Harvey)

Osgood House Hotel, Cookshire, Que. (www.stampauctionnetwork.com)

Ken and Susie were married in November 1928 at the historic little St. Barnabus Anglican Church in Lake Megantic, which celebrated its centenary in 1991. Ken's sister, Maude, and her husband, Herbert Patton, were their witnesses and gave them a beautiful mantle clock as a wedding gift. The clock told time for more than 60 years at the Dew Drop Inn and is presently in the loving care of their granddaughter, Kerri Fraser.

Ken and Susie's marriage certificate, 1928 (Fraser family archives)

In the beginning

Ken and Susie marriage civil return, 1928 (Fraser family archives)

Susie and Ken at St. Barnabus Church, Lac Mégantic, Que., 1991 (Fraser family archives)

Following their marriage Ken and Susie moved to Sherbrooke, where they lived in an upper-floor apartment on Mount Pleasant Street. Not long afterwards, they were blessed with their first bundle of joy — a baby girl they named Mabel. Her brother, Charles, who would not be born until seven years later, recalls a story their mom told him about Mabel soon after she learned to walk:

Mantle clock wedding gift (Courtesy of Kerri Fraser)

Susie and baby Mabel (Courtesy of Johnny Scholes)

In the beginning

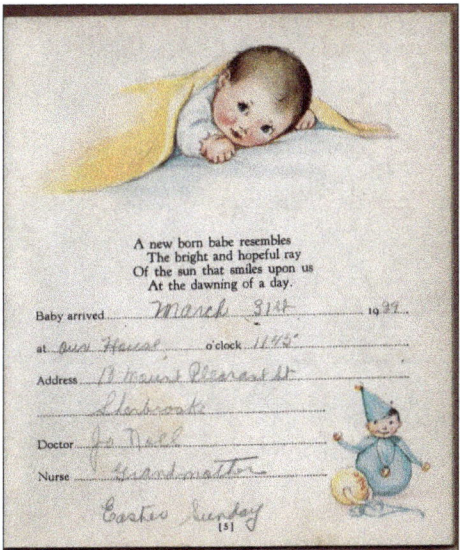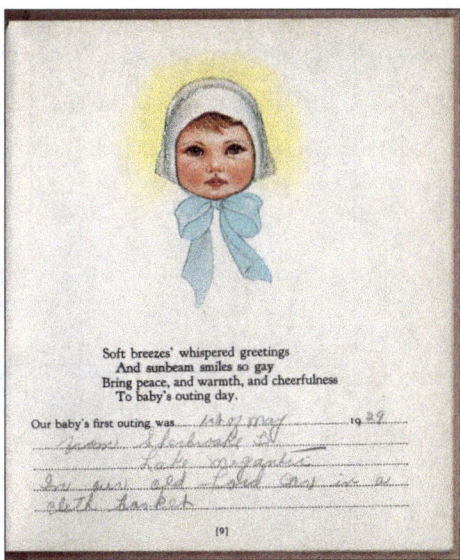

Mabel Fraser baby book – birth details (left) and first trip away (right) (Fraser family archives)

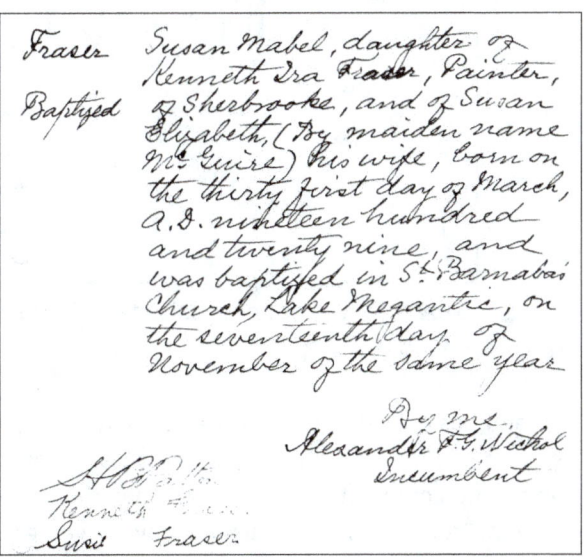

Mabel Susan Fraser baptismal document, 1929 (www.ancestry.com)

The second floor tenement where they lived had an outdoor balcony. One day, Mom looked out and was horrified to see that Mabel had climbed up over the railing and was holding on to the outside of the posts. Fearing that Mabel would lose her grip and fall to the ground below, she avoided shouting in order not to startle the little girl. So she quickly and quietly went out onto the balcony and rescued Mabel. But it frightened my parents terribly. (Charles W.K. Fraser)

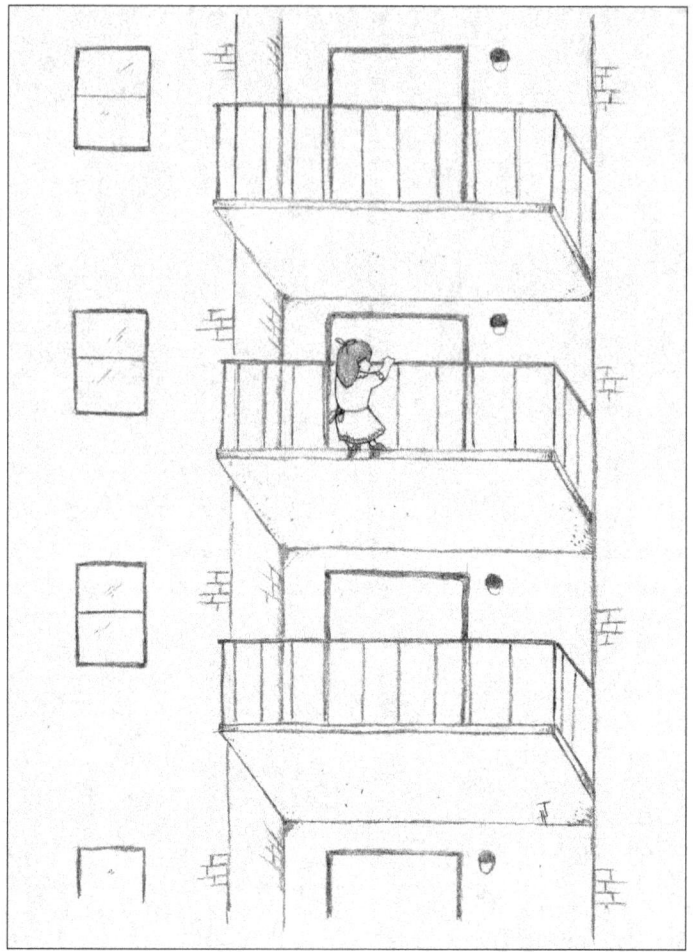

Baby Mabel climbs over balcony railing (Sketch by James Harvey)

Ken and Susie lived in Sherbrooke for only a couple of years, during which time Ken worked as a painter and as a labourer on the railroad roundhouse construction or maintenance project. Then they moved to Cookshire and launched the Dew Drop Inn. And what a bold move it was, given that it was the beginning of the Great Depression. Writing in the December 2008 issue of the Fraser Family Link, nephew Jim Fraser comments: "Launching a new business and making it successful during the Great Depression required much hard work, perseverance and resourcefulness."

The remaining chapters of this book relate the multi-faceted story of Ken and Susie's Dew Drop Inn as remembered by family, friends and acquaintances.

Chapter 2   Room at the inn

Dew Drop Inn postcard, circa 1935 (Courtesy of Roger Dionne)

The building

The building that was to become known as the Dew Drop Inn was not an especially attractive structure. In fact it was quite nondescript. It lacked the beauty and majesty of some other buildings in town, such as the Cromwell and Pope residences. However, once Susie decorated it with flowerboxes and Ken applied some paint and dressed it up with advertising signs, it was a pretty darned good-looking place!

Built during the mid-1800s, it had most recently served as a haberdashery or millinery store, selling hats and other clothing accessories. Probably the building once housed a tailor shop as well, because according to son Charles, the word TAILOR used to be written on the east side of the building. In any case, Ken and Susie bought the building in May 1930 from a Mr. John Planche, who had a reputation as being somewhat of a wheeler-dealer in real estate. Charles explains:

> Dad had the feeling that Mr. Planche was always waiting for him to miss a payment. He was known to provide mortgages to people and then seize the property immediately if they missed a single payment. He was

also known for his stinginess. Dad would send him the payment by mail but Planche would wait until Mabel came home from school to give her the receipt so that he could save the cost of the two-cent stamp! (Charles W.K. Fraser)

Corner of Main and Craig streets, Cookshire, 1935 (Courtesy of Almon Pope)

Dew Drop Inn postcard, circa 1945. Right: text on the backside (Courtesy of Christopher Standish)

DEW DROP INN
Cookshire, Quebec, Canada.
on Routes 27-28.
Meals, Lunches and Refreshments
Rooms for Tourists, Bath and Shower.
Kenneth Fraser, Prop.

Dew Drop Inn, circa 1960 (Photo by author)

Charles describes the layout of the upstairs area: "The Inn had six rooms upstairs and two summer rooms out over the shed." The Cookshire Centennial 1892-1992 book notes that in its early years the Dew Drop Inn provided accommodation for 10 to 15 guests.

The first floor space was shared between the store and the restaurant. When the Dew Drop Inn opened for business, the store's very first customer was prominent Cookshire businessman Lester Wootten, who would later become mayor. Apparently he came in and bought a pack of cigarettes to encourage the new business in town.

The restaurant area initially consisted of a few small tables arranged around the walls with a larger table in the center of the room. Later on, booths replaced the tables. During its busiest years, up to fifty meals a day were served at the Dew Drop Inn.

Following are some additional memories of various physical aspects of the Dew Drop Inn building and property:

> When you went up the stairs, you could make a left and there were two guest rooms out in there, you went down two steps, that was towards the garage, but if you went the other way, all the way in, there were two guest rooms on the left hand side also. And on the right hand side were

Dew Drop Inn

A landmark of Cookshire for the last sixty years.

In May of 1930, Ken & Susie Fraser bought a building at 30 Main Street West. The place had at one time housed a Millenery Shop at the ground floor and was home of the Local Radio Club on the 2nd floor.

Ken and Susie opened a business that was to be known as DEW DROP INN. They not only served meals, but provided rooms for travelers and tourists. In those early years, they served as many as fifty meals a day and offered beds for ten to fifteen people at night.

DEW DROP INN

During the second world war, business declined and it was then that Kenneth started driving taxi with is "Hudsons's". Susie got into "Hairdressing" service which still continues to this day.

The DEW DROP INN was also home to "Shell" gas for over forty five years. The first pump for service was of the manual type and stood ten feet high in front of the house.

During low periods, Ken painted numerous signs "free-hand". His work was very appreciated.

The place is still open. Even today you can buy chocolates, cards and souvenirs at the DEW DROP INN and be served either by Ken or by Susie.

Dew Drop Inn profile in the Cookshire Centennial book, 1992

Room at the inn

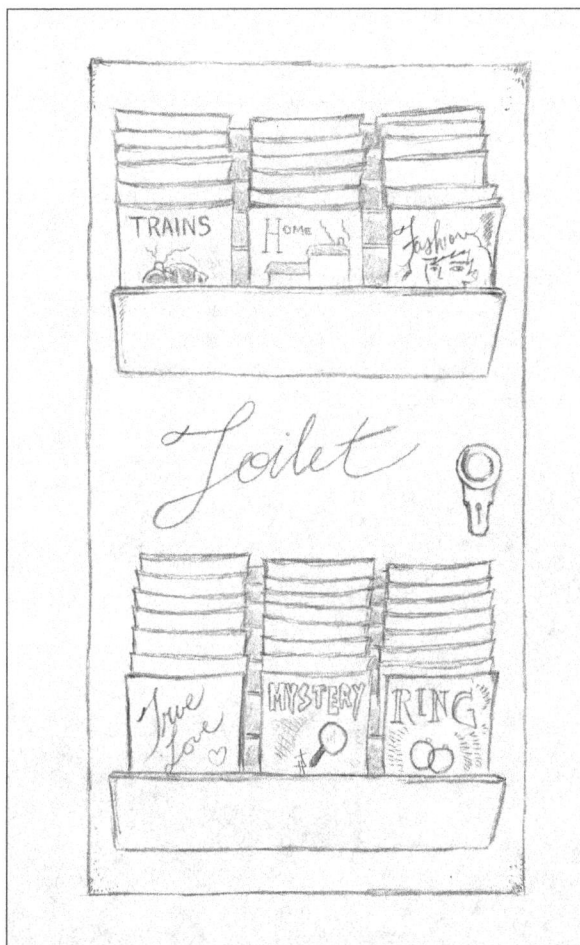

Dew Drop Inn's loo library (Sketch by James Harvey)

Rooms sign at front steps
(Fraser family archives)

Ken and Susie's room and Charles's room. When Mabel moved out, they made her room into a guest room. (Bobbie Bowen)

On the door to the washroom, as well as on the walls inside, were a ton of magazines and clippings about sports, trains, news – everything. So when you went to the bathroom, you could read in there for an hour! (Bobbie Bowen)

Upstairs there was a door with a hole in it – like a little trap door. Apparently the Radio Society met there and they had some kind of secret process to gain access. Members were those people who had the first radios in Cookshire. Dad was not a member but he had a very old radio that was there when he bought the building. He made a sign that said something like "SILENCE PLEASE" to prevent conversation while the radio was on because of its very low sound volume. (Charles W.K. Fraser)

I remember the telephone booth behind the counter. Having a couple of girlfriends over the course of my Cookshire High School days, I would go down to Ken's and use his telephone booth for my lengthy chatting sessions. (Almon Pope)

I remember the very steep steps to get up to the main floor. (Frasier Bellam)

I remember Uncle Ken's recycled calendar on the wall. He would save old calendars and when the same configuration of days within the months would repeat several years later, he would reuse them! Of course the year was wrong but that didn't matter since all the months were correct. (Kevin Ross)

I remember the shed out back, next to a butternut tree, that we used for a "camp." I also remember Ken's garage that was connected to the house. The Ellyson girls, my sister Megan and I found old magazines back there. Ken had inscribed weather data over probably something like 20 years on the wall. (Alexandra Pope)

Alexandra Pope at her camp behind Dew Drop Inn, circa 1972 (Courtesy of Almon Pope)

I saw these weather inscriptions myself and remember that there were entries of temperatures, rainfall amounts and things such as the season's first snow or winter snowstorm accumulations, etc. This data was pencilled on the door with, if my memory serves me well, a carpenter's pencil. (Almon Pope)

The Dew Drop Inn building sat on a very narrow piece of property. In fact, it seems that almost no land came with the purchase of the building. It was basically the building itself and the land on which it sat. A neighbouring house, also owned by Mr. Planche, sat on the adjoining property just above the Dew Drop Inn. Many years later, in 1959, Ken and Susie had the opportunity to buy this adjacent property, as noted in Mabel's diary entry:

> May 19, 1959: Rufus (Cromwell) phoned saying we could buy Planche's house if we wanted to. (Mabel Fraser's diary)

Charles explains the outcome of Mr. Planche's offer: "Dad didn't buy the Planche house right away. Don MacRae, who was working at nearby Hurd's Meat Market, bought it. He bought both the house and the property between it and the Dew Drop Inn. Then my mom got involved because she realized that it would be a good property to have. So they worked out an arrangement with Don MacRae to acquire the land between them to go with the Dew Drop Inn."

The name

It is not known with certainty how Ken and Susie chose the name for their new home and business. Perhaps they were taking a romantic evening stroll in the dew-laden grass when they invented the name. Or maybe Susie had suggested "Do Drop In" as the name but Ken misinterpreted it when he painted the big sign that hung out front! But the most likely theory is that they had seen the name used elsewhere and liked it so much that they decided to adopt it for their enterprise.

Before doing the research for this book, I, like most Townshippers, believed that Cookshire was home to the ONE AND ONLY Dew Drop Inn. However, I was very wrong. In fact, there are scores – if not hundreds – of entities (businesses, organizations, media, etc.) in Canada, the U.S.A. and around the world that operate under this revered moniker! Below is a sampling of the imposters that I discovered through a simple non-exhaustive Google search:

- Dew Drop Inn: a cozy little Irish pub in Galway, Ireland
- The Alaska, Dawson Creek's oldest standing hotel, which opened its doors to guests in 1931 as the "Dew Drop Inn"
- Dew Drop Inn B&B, 22 km northeast of Lac La Biche, Alta.
- Dew Drop Inn, Saranac Lake, N.Y.
- A musical group named Dew Drop Inn
- "Holiday at the Dew Drop Inn," the third and final book in the series by Eve Garnett
- Dew Drop Inn soup kitchen, Thunder Bay, Ont.
- Dew Drop Inn, Woolloomooloo, Australia (now known as East Sydney)
- The first Kentucky Fried Chicken outlet, the former Dew Drop Inn in Salt Lake City, Utah
- Dew Drop Inn, a film released in 1919 and directed by Larry Semon
- Dew Drop Inn, advertised as "Mobile's oldest restaurant," in Mobile, Alabama

Dew Drop Inn

Of course, Dew Drop Inn is also a clever and cute play on words. An article by M. Segal in a 1984 issue of the McGill Journal of Education analyzes this precise phrase from a technical literary perspective:

> Many puns. . . are ambiguous in more than one way. The name of the motel, the Dew Drop Inn, for example, combines syntactic ("drop" and "inn") and phonologieal-syntactie ("dew") ambiguity, and it is at the same time a homophonie ("inn"), a homographic ("drop") and a phonemie ("dew") pun.

The location

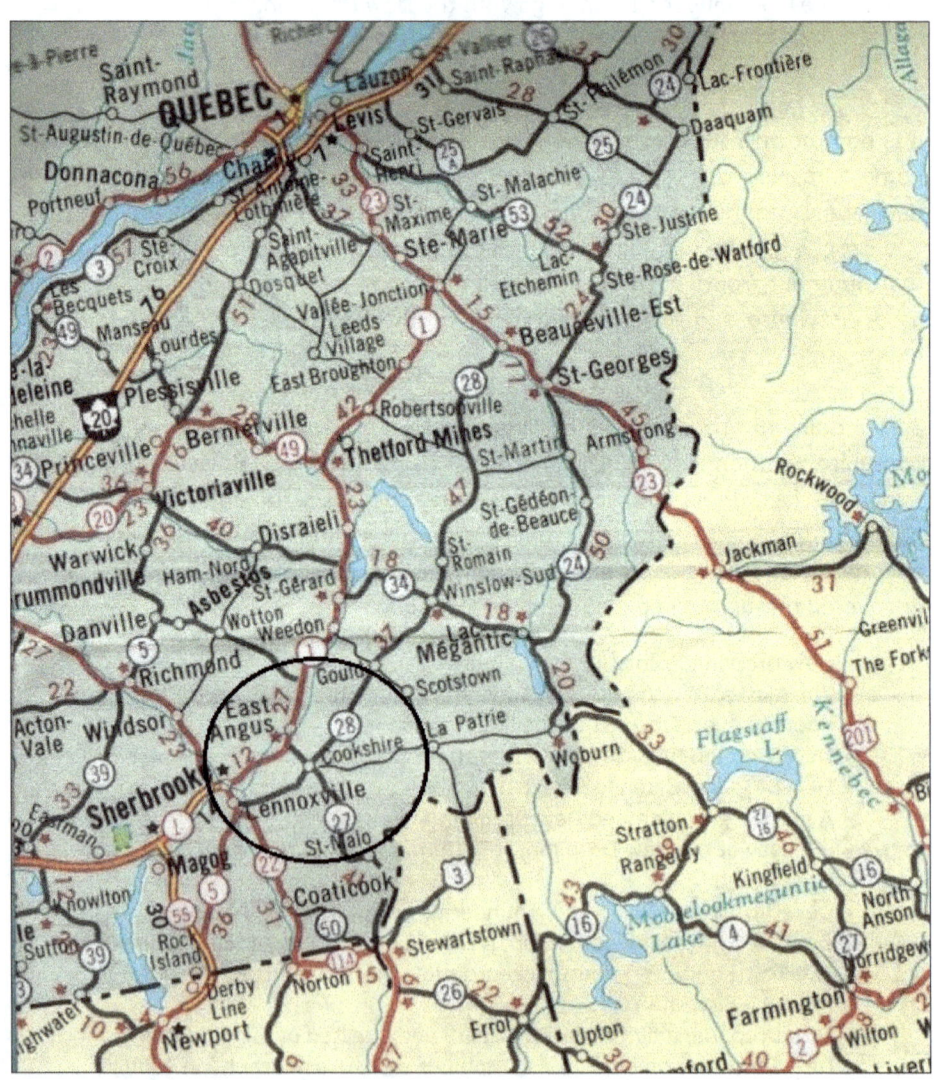

1972 Quebec map showing Cookshire at the intersection of routes 27 and 28

Room at the inn

In the glory days of the Dew Drop Inn, Cookshire was ideally located for the tourist trade, as expressed in the two following items:

> The Dew Drop Inn was strategically located at the junction of two of the oldest highways of the Eastern Townships and was a reminder that we would soon be home. There was a lot of activity in this part of town. There was a hotel across from where the post office is today. Beside it was a grocery store where they maple-smoked the meat. Mr. Fraser also sold gas. The Anglican Church was just across the street. In a nutshell, it was located in the heart of an Eastern Townships village built on the banks of an old salmon river, the Eaton, where the Indigenous peoples practiced their traditions much earlier. This region, particularly near Lac Mégantic, contains the oldest traces of First Nations settlements anywhere in Canada, going back 11,000 years. The history of British colonization and the resulting presence of Mr. Fraser and the Dew Drop Inn in this territory are thus very recent. (Jean-François Nadeau, Cookshire native, historian and author)

> Cookshire is built on the western slope of the valley of the Eaton River, and commands a fine view of one of the most picturesque sections of the Province of Quebec. One of the most popular highways leading from the New England States into the province and on to Quebec City passes through the village and affords the tourists glimpses of water and landscape views of rare charm and beauty. (Excerpt from an unidentified 1933 newspaper article entitled "Cookshire Nestles Peacefully Amid Picturesque Surroundings.")

St. Peters Church and Rectory (Photo by author)

Neighbours Fred and Mary Noble's house, on the site of the current post office (Photo by author)

Dew Drop Inn and Hurd's Meat Market (Courtesy of Almon Pope)

Room at the inn

John Cook covered bridge on the Eaton River (Photo by author)

The guests

The Dew Drop Inn's clientele consisted mainly of tourists who were passing through town, travelling salesmen who came to pedal their wares, and friends and relatives who kept returning to enjoy the matchless Fraser hospitality. Below are some of the memories shared by others about the Inn's guests.

> I remember there used to be a lot of American tourists. (Louise Knox)

> A lot of people would stop for gas and then, realizing that it was an inn, would have meals and stay overnight. (Charles W.K. Fraser)

> There would be a travelling salesman once in a while. I would go up and stay there for two to three weeks at a time. (Bobbie Bowen)

> Cousins Doris and Rudy Carlson would come up from Massachusetts and stay at Dew Drop Inn while visiting relatives in the area. (Gloria Bellam)

> Mr. and Mrs. Sargent were regular guests for several years. (Rodger Heatherington)

> Ken and Susie had friends stay there but I really didn't know of anyone personally. However, I'm sure of one thing – guests would have been treated like royalty. (Rev. Ron West)

> During the Depression, different families – maybe husband and wife and perhaps a child – would come and get their lodging free in exchange for helping Dad with something. (Charles W.K. Fraser)

> I was impressed by the homeliness of all the people that came and went. You never knew who'd come through the front door. (Bobbie Bowen)

The inn portion of the business declined during the 1950s as new highways were built and motels gained in popularity. Around 1960, Dew Drop Inn ceased to be an inn but the restaurant and general store continued for another 20 or 30 years.

The staff

In normal times, Ken and Susie, with the help of their children Mabel and Charles, carried the lion's share of the duties associated with running an inn. Close friends and visiting relatives would also lend a hand. But in peak times, when business was booming, additional staff was required. One of those hired was my own mother, Alice Hood, who worked there for a couple of years in the early 1930s. In fact, it was there that she met my dad, Ken's older brother. Apparently my dad would make very frequent visits to Dew Drop Inn, ostensibly to buy a pack of his favourite teaberry gum!

One of my mom's stories of her time working at the Dew Drop Inn involves how she "freshened up" hotdogs that perhaps had passed their "best before" dates – by trimming off any traces of mould. Although this may sound rather shocking, it must be remembered that was during the Depression when money was scarce and nothing was wasted.

Following is a summary of others' recollections of Dew Drop Inn staff, some of whom would become lifelong friends of the family.

> My dad, Mac Sr. ("Jack"), worked at the Dew Drop in the 1930s, and that is where the long-lasting friendship between our families began. (Malcolm "Mac" MacLeod)

> Jack MacLeod came to work for Dad from up in Lake Megantic. There is an interesting story about how he asked for and got the job. Jack drove an old car and wore his cap pulled way down over his eyes. One day he drove up to the pumps and asked Dad for a gallon or two of gas – a very, very little amount. Before pumping the gas, Dad walked back around to ask him if he had any money. Jack said that he had just enough for a gallon or two and that he was looking for a job. So Dad hired him on the spot in exchange for room, board and cigarettes. Jack worked in the store, served lunch and did all kinds of work. Dad said that he was the best worker he ever had and that he did the most business during the time that Jack was working there. (Charles W.K. Fraser)

Room at the inn

Above: An unidentified friend outside Dew Drop Inn, circa 1940 (Fraser family archives)

Right: Alice Hood Fraser, circa 1933 (Fraser family archives)

Ken and Susie hired a woman who did chores around the kitchen. I can't think of her name. She would also cook when they weren't around. Otherwise, if they were busy, she would make sure that everything was cleaned and put away. That was back when I was 10 or 11 years old (around 1945). They were very busy in those years. Later on, when all the new places like McDonald's began appearing, it had a very negative impact on the Dew Drop Inn's business. And the building of a new highway to Quebec City didn't help either. (Bobbie Bowen)

As a kid, I remember working in the Inn – bringing in suitcases. I never stopped. I don't know if I was too young or not but I worked all the time. Sometimes I would get a nickel for a tip. But the chances weren't even 50-50 that you would get a tip – it was very much hit or miss. (Charles W.K. Fraser)

Mom lived at the Dew Drop Inn when she worked there as both cook and chambermaid. (John "Jack" Fraser)

Georgie Coates and Ruth Miller also worked there as waitresses. Somebody might ask Georgie for an egg sandwich and she would tell the kitchen that they wanted a hamburger! She couldn't remember too well, and for a long time she would not write things down. But finally she would write the orders down all the time. (Charles W.K. Fraser)

Dew Drop Inn

My sister Marilyn MacRae worked in the restaurant one summer. I also worked there for two or three summers, as well as after school and sometimes on weekends. It was a great experience and I learned a lot from both Ken and Susie. Of course I was mercilessly teased by Ken! (Betty MacRae Wright)

Ken and Susie with family and friends, circa 1940 (Courtesy of Mac MacLeod)

Inn operating license, 1944
(Courtesy of Charles W.K. Fraser)

Chapter 3 Eat, drink and be merry

Dew Drop Inn menu (Courtesy of Kerri Fraser)

Although Cookshire in the good old days had other restaurants such as the Green Lantern and the Royal Café, none of them quite matched the Dew Drop Inn in terms of selection, service or, most of all, atmosphere. Where else could you find such an attractive array of freshly-fried fat-free fast food? And where else could you find such a friendly waiter as Ken Fraser, who entertained guests with a constant stream of spontaneous stories? And where else could you enjoy a delicious meal in the nearby presence of men playing cribbage or a dog sprawled on the table of the adjoining booth, waiting for something to bark at? Nowhere else could come close to offering such an awesome ambiance. The Dew Drop Inn was indeed a unique place to eat!

Meals

An early handwritten slightly dog-eared menu, probably dating to the 1940s, contains the following hot meal main course meat dishes:

- hamburg steak $0.70
- sausage $0.60
- fried ham $0.75
- ham & eggs $1.00
- chicken pie $1.35
- sirloin steak $1.50
- pork chop $0.70
- cold ham $0.60
- bacon & eggs $0.90
- (SPECIAL) spaghetti & tomato sauce $0.50

Window sign, circa 1938 (Courtesy of Bobbie Bowen)

No less than a dozen different types of sandwiches were offered, ranging in price from $0.15 for peanut butter to $0.45 for ham & egg. Three types of omelets were available, starting at $0.50. If you wished to include a salad, of which there were six options, it would cost an additional $0.60 to $1.00.

The dessert menu was equally tempting. A piece of one of Susie's home-baked pies cost only $0.15, while a banana split was $0.40. Beverages included tea, coffee, milk, Postum, Bovril and hot chocolate (no prices indicated – they were probably included with the meal).

The list of beverages is rather curious for a couple of reasons. Firstly, it includes a drink that may be unfamiliar to many. Postum is a powdered roasted-grain beverage that was popular as a coffee substitute during World War II, when coffee was rationed. Secondly, soft drinks were totally absent from the list. Perhaps they weren't considered as appropriate liquid accompaniment for Dew Drop Inn cuisine. In any case, this subject will be addressed more fully in the next section.

Meals were even cheaper in the 1930s as evidenced by a sign in the window that advertised "Regular Meals" for 40 cents and up.

Personally, I never had the pleasure of eating a meal at the Dew Drop Inn, so I have to rely on the experiences of those who have. Following is a sampling of their recollections:

> My earliest memory was having the noon meal at the Dew Drop Inn on my first day of school. (Ben Hodge)
>
> When I was 5 or 6, I had breakfast at Dew Drop Inn with my sister and father. (Muriel French Fitzsimmons)
>
> When I was growing up, this was one of the highlights of our trips to town. Mom would take us there for lunch. We used to sit in one of the

Eat, drink and be merry

booths and watch the cars coming in for gas, while we enjoyed the best tasting hot dog I have ever eaten. Mr. Fraser was never too busy to answer questions or simply talk about the weather. This is one of my fondest childhood memories. (Norma Wiley)

I can still see Ken when I would go to the restaurant for lunch, as he usually prepared the lunch orders. I can still see him coming out of the kitchen to the end of the restaurant counter, with raw hamburg in his hand pressing it into shape for a hamburger. (Muriel Watson)

Susie was a marvellous cook. (Louise Knox)

When I would come downstairs at 7:30 or 8 o'clock Susie had already made two tins of biscuits and a couple of pies! (Bobbie Bowen)

At times, Susie would get me to help her. I would carry stuff from the kitchen to the little tables in the restaurant. (Louise Knox)

Ken was the waiter. And if someone wanted something cold such as a ham sandwich, he would prepare it for them. But if they wanted a cooked meal, Susie would do it. (Bobbie Bowen)

January 10, 1959: Made two apple pie puddings in the afternoon, good as always. (Mabel Fraser's diary)

Johnny McInally would eat meals at the Dew Drop Inn on a fairly regular basis. I remember the great smell of Susie's cooking. In her absence, Ken would prepare the odd meal – albeit Susie's cooking re-heated. Later on, as I moved about, I would eat there – my favourite dish was Susie's macaroni and meat. (Almon Pope)

Charlie Ross always ate lunch when in the area, as did several school bus drivers, and, of course, Doug Twyman, who worked at Hurd's Meat Market next door. (Rodger Heatherington)

Austin Young, a 102-year-old resident of Willowdale Retirement Center in Smith Falls, Ont. where I worked, was originally from Stanstead-Rock Island and told me that he remembers eating at the Dew Drop Inn. (Karen Fraser Jackson)

Regular diner John McInally (Courtesy of Mac MacLeod)

The Fairbairn brothers (Bruce and Derek), who were servers at St. Peter's Church, would join Almon ("Fred") Pope and the Lagacé brothers (Jack and Jim) for breakfast. Aunt Susie would hurry home from singing in the choir to cook and serve the meal for them. (Jim Fraser)

July 9, 1959: Two guys in for lunch. San and I split the 10 cent tip. . . Split another 10 cent tip. (Mabel Fraser's diary)

I remember that they had a couple of cats and a big German shepherd dog that would lie on the table until someone came in to eat. Then Ken would coax him down, wipe off the table and seat the customer for their meal! (Bob Taylor)

On one bitter cold winter day as we were heading home for lunch, Aunt Susie came out and said, "You children (i.e., Marina, June and John) must come in and have dinner with us." We were very excited and the meal was delicious, but unfortunately Mom and Dad hadn't been told about it so we were in trouble when we got home. (June Fraser Patterson)

From when I first came to Cookshire, when I first got to know Ken and Susie, there were a number of issues that we had to deal with. And one of them was that we were getting people coming to my house asking for lunch or for something like that. I talked to Ken and Susie about it because they were still offering lunch at that time. So, from then on, any time someone came to my door asking for something to eat, I would send them over to the Dew Drop Inn telling them "You go eat over there and I'll take care of the bill." (Rev. Ron West)

Drinks

Directly behind the counter was a very large cooler that contained a variety of soft drinks, including Coke, Pepsi, Orange Crush, root beer, Bryant's Bull's Head Ginger Ale and many more. Ordering a soft drink at the Dew Drop Inn was normally a simple procedure, but there were two exceptions. Ken would have a special reaction whenever a person asked for Coke or Pepsi. Someone who experienced this first-hand shares her memories:

Uncle Ken called Coca Cola "Big Poison" and Pepsi "Little Poison." Any customer who ordered them would receive a lecture on the dangerous effects of these beverages. I remember believing that Coca Cola was practically sinful and I was truly afraid to ever drink it. He also described it as poison to some of my friends when they'd buy it, and warned them of the horrible disaster it would create in one's stomach. (Marilyn Fraser Reed)

I also took my uncle's warnings very seriously and avoided Coke and Pepsi like the plague. To this day, I have never consumed an ounce of either of them. Over the years, my siblings and I have laughed at our uncle's "Big Poison" and "Little Poison" monikers. At the same time, we were puzzled as to why he would sell these drinks if they were so dangerous.

Eat, drink and be merry

Recent research by reputable organizations indicates that Ken's characterization of these popular drinks was much more accurate than we had imagined. Various studies have shown a link between the consumption of such drinks and an increased incidence of obesity, diabetes, heart disease, osteoporosis and other health problems. It is these three ingredients of Coke and Pepsi that are individually and collectively responsible: sugar, caffeine and phosphoric acid. The major difference between colas and other carbonated beverages is that the caffeine and phosphoric acid are not present in other soft drinks. One article stated "Coke is poison and is used for cleaning rust and toilets – its acidity level matches that of battery acid." and another said "A sugary drink is like poison for your body." So it appears that Ken was right after all!

Coke and obese Santa (by David Parkins, www.bloomberg.com)

In the Dew Drop Inn era, dépanneurs (convenience stores) in Quebec were not permitted to sell wine or beer. But even if they had been allowed to, it is a virtual certainty that Ken Fraser would not have stocked such products. He was strongly opposed to drinking alcoholic beverages of any kind. This attitude had deep roots in the Fraser family. Ken's great-aunt, Fannie Rankin Fraser, was a member of the Women's Christian Temperance Union and signed a formal pledge in 1875 never to drink alcohol. According to Ken's cousin, Gloria Frasier Bellam, other family members were asked to sign similar pledges.

As a seller of soft drinks, Dew Drop Inn also took back the empty bottles, paying between two and five cents apiece, depending on the size. A young summer visitor to Cookshire recounts her experience of collecting "empties" and cashing them in at Ken's store.

> A long day stretches ahead of us in Cookshire. It is bright and sunny, and full of delicious possibilities. Hmmmm. We think we will make it truly delicious. Laura, Gordie and I head outside, each with a paper bag, to hunt for soft-drink bottles. We are in Quebec, in the 1950s, and there is absolutely no concept of recycling or ecology. Have a full ashtray as you travel? Open the window and shake. Empty lunch bags as you wend your way along the roads? Fling them out the window. But that is just useless garbage. What interests us is the money-making trash. For every bottle we find, we will get two cents. And two cents times a few bottles will buy us a lot of penny candy at the Cookshire general stores. We head down the hill to the lower part of town, where there is the most traffic. We carefully pick our way through the ditches. In no time at all we each have

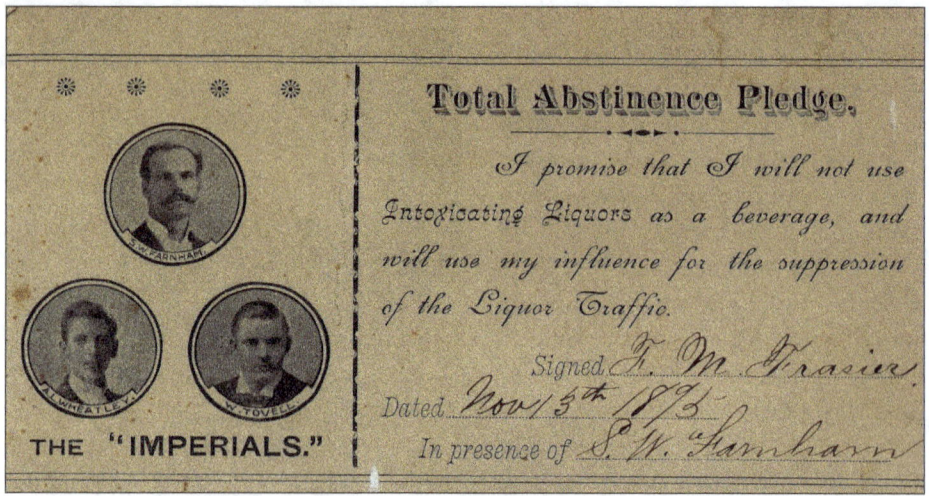

Fannie Rankin Frasier's Total Abstinence Pledge (Fraser family archives)

> our bag half-full. Fine. That is all we want. Enough to satisfy...Now, which store will we go to? We can go to Pope's, on the main crossroads of town, or up the street just a little to Ken's. We choose Ken's, as we almost always do. His store, which has been here since Mom was a little girl, is called Dew Drop Inn. It is dark, full of all kinds of clutter, and has two tables by the front windows. One table usually has his German shepherd lying on it, looking out the window. The other often has men gathered around it as they play cribbage. Dad usually comes to play when he is in town...But, much as I love poking around in the scary dark rows at the back of the store, today I am interested only in the candy – jars and jars of it in front of the cash register . . . black balls, three for a penny; strawberries, two for a penny; lollipops and double bubble . . . Ken teases us as he always does – will never call us by our real names, though he knows them well, but always "Priscilla!" (Barbara Challies)

Another of the Dew Drop Inn's beverages, hot chocolate, has a heart-warming story associated with it.

> I was born and raised in East Angus. What I remember about the Dew Drop Inn are the sleigh rides from the East Angus High School. We were in our early teens and Clifford Cameron or Lawrence Kinnear drove us. Sometimes we got off the sleigh, walked a while, and threw snowballs at each other. Then we'd have to run to catch up to the sleigh. If we were cold, there were always blankets on the sleigh to warm us up. My sister Sheila remembers these rides well, also Buddy Stickles and Sonny Knapp whom he phoned in B.C. He remembered that someone called ahead to the Dew Drop Inn to say that we were coming. Everyone fondly remembers the warm restaurant with free hot chocolate waiting for us. We used to buy stuff to eat as Ken seemed to have everything in his store. Sonny remembers going upstairs to see the electric trains that

Eat, drink and be merry

went very fast. Ken and Susie always made us feel welcome. We always looked forward to those sleigh rides. The roads were not plowed then as they are today. We were happy to have these rides to look forward to. Today we couldn't. (Jean Evans)

Heading for free hot chocolate at Dew Drop Inn (Sketch by James Harvey)

Ice cream

From its giant hand-painted billboards along the roads leading into Cookshire and from its big storefront sign, Dew Drop Inn loudly and proudly proclaimed that it had THE BEST ICE CREAM IN TOWN. And that it did! As a once-a-week purchaser of a double scoop of vanilla for five cents, I can attest to the quality of this treat that for me served as an appetizer while walking home after Sunday Church to Mom's ham stew dinner. Although vanilla was always my personal favourite, there were several other flavours to choose from, including chocolate, strawberry, cherry, Neapolitan, maple walnut and probably half a dozen more. Not quite the 40 or more flavours offered by Ben and Jerry's today, but still a great selection for back then. I recall one day when I was chatting with Uncle Ken, a guy came in and asked "What kind of ice cream do you have?" After my uncle rhymed off his complete list of flavours, the guy asked, "Do you have green gooseberry?" Uncle Ken would later tell me that this guy always asked for a flavour he didn't have!

Dew Drop Inn

Hunting's Dairy sign (www.patrimoineduquebec.com)

The Dew Drop Inn's ice cream always came from Hunting's Dairy in Huntingville, Que. (now part of Sherbrooke). It came in large 2-gallon tubs that were stored in a special ice cream freezer where each flavour had its own separate compartment whose lid closed with a loud "thud." Although cones was initially the most popular way that ice cream was sold, popsicles, fudgicles and ice cream sandwiches later joined the product line. It was also sold in one pound "bricks." But whatever form it took, Dew Drop Inn's ice cream was a favourite for many, as evidenced by the following recollections.

In the summer I think most of the kids headed to Dew Drop Inn to buy popsicles or ice cream. (Eleanor Vogell Twyman)

Our Sunday treat was when my uncle would take us down to the Dew Drop Inn to pick up a brick of ice cream. (Bob Taylor)

I would go to the Dew Drop Inn for an ice cream cone with my grandmother. (Dorothy Shelton Dionne)

I remember going there for an ice cream cone while attending Cookshire High School. (Muriel Watson)

I remember buying Hunting's fruit ice cream cones. (Rodger Heatherington)

I would buy an ice cream sandwich or a 10-cent bag of potato chips during the obligatory stop-in after Church. (Jim Fraser)

I sometimes worked behind the counter serving people who came in for ice cream. (Bobbie Bowen)

July 9, 1959: Dad to Huntingville and Sherbrooke at 1:30. *(no doubt for Hunting's Dairy ice cream)* (Mabel Fraser's diary)

Candies galore

Because candies clearly cannot be classified as a food, one might question their inclusion in this chapter. However it can be justified based on a broad interpretation of the chapter's title, "Eat, drink and be merry." Since candies certainly make children "merry," their inclusion here can definitely be considered appropriate.

To children who either grew up in Cookshire or came to visit, Dew Drop Inn was synonymous with candies. Even if they recall nothing else about the place, they

Eat, drink and be merry

remember the huge selection of candies as well as chocolates, peppermints and bubble-gum. And the occasional lack of freshness of some of these items didn't seem to matter. Several long-ago kids of Cookshire share their "sweet" Dew Drop Inn memories here:

> My first memories are probably from the mid 1950s. Walking to the post office to pick up mail necessitated passing by the Dew Drop Inn and its treasure trove of candies. Of course we would spend considerable time to spend our few cents wisely. Different candies cost different amounts and some were a real bargain, like 3 for 1 cent. I remember the "Jaw Breakers." They were covered in a sooty black layer that was unpleasant and covered your mouth in black. But then it was followed by multiple tasty layers that changed colour. As the name suggests, they were very hard and hence lasted a long time. Now that's a name that legal-minded marketers would not use today, but for us it was quite tempting and daring. On special occasions we would spend a whole five cents on a small bag of BBQ potato chips. That was a real treat. The shop had many marvellous things including toys, sundries, newspapers, but to a 10-year-old the candy was the star attraction. I wonder now if that precious little brown bag of candies we got at the Christmas party in the Church Hall across the street came from Dew Drop Inn. (Dr. Emily Hamilton)

We moved next door to the Dew Drop Inn in 1947 when I was seven years old. My earliest memory was that I had found candy paradise. We were actually allowed to go behind the counter and choose what we wanted from all the penny candy. Then Ken would count them out and make little comments about our choices. (Betty MacRae Wright)

I remember the glass-topped bins with all sorts of candies and sweets. (Norma Wiley)

Dew Drop Inn's gumball dispenser (Courtesy of Kerri Fraser)

I used to stop by Ken's after school or on weekends to buy Opeechee Bubble gum (mostly for the hockey cards that were enclosed together with a flat piece of gum). The cards were popular at school at the time (1960s) and we used to flick them against the school basement walls. The card that landed closest to the wall took all. I would be allowed behind the counter near the door to get my own jawbreaker gum and liquorice. I remember that the gum was always soft, thanks to one of Ken's cats that liked to sleep on top of the gum in its box. Usually the liquorice would have a few cat hairs attached

Left: Jawbreaker candy (ref. www.vikaljija.com)
Right: Bazooka Joe bubblegum package (ref. www.dvdbash.com)

but we ate it anyway! The word was out not to buy any Smiles 'n Chuckles chocolate bars because they were really old, so we kids avoided them. (Almon Pope)

I bought candy and maybe a chocolate if it wasn't **too** old! (Dorothy Ross)

I remember going down there from school and buying candies for little or nothing. (Barbara Keys Lassenba)

Uncle Ken always had a container with loose candy – probably broken packages. There were Lifesavers and hard candy, two for one cent. I loved the delicious bullet-hard white candies for one cent. I only found out years later they were really marshmallows that had hardened with age! (June Fraser Patterson)

I remember going into Uncle Ken's almost every night with some of my school friends. One of us was sure to have a penny so we could buy those three-for-one-cent black balls and the other two-for-one-cent candies. If we were lucky, we'd buy those two-cent liquorice pipes, which we were forbidden to smoke but which were acceptable if we ate them as if they were candy. From time to time, if we went in alone, Uncle Ken would give us free Chicklets or an entire box of "aged" chocolates. (Marilyn Fraser Reed)

I bought Bazooka bubble gum or two-for-a-penny licorice balls. (Frasier Bellam)

I recall receiving my hard-earned weekly allowance – was it two cents or five cents? – and taking it into Dew Drop Inn and buying jellybeans or gumdrops from those big candy jars on the counter. (John "Jack" Fraser)

In my younger years, I remember going behind the counter and trying to make a big decision – which candy to buy? There were too many choices. The blackballs were a big hit. (Karen Fraser Jackson)

Vintage box of Smiles 'n Chuckles chocolates (www.terapeak.com)

After Miss Elliott released me, I remember popping in to the Dew Drop for a two-Chicklet gum box, licorice pipe, or Bazooka Joe bubble gum with the cartoon strip. If I was alone, often the candy would be free. (Warren Fraser)

When I was a child, Ken would sometimes give me extra candy or bubble-gum when I went in with a few pennies to spend. (Dorothy Shelton Dionne)

Vintage heart-shaped box of Ganong's chocolates (Author's collection)

I remember the Smiles 'n Chuckles chocolate bar glass showcase. (Almon Pope)

Dew Drop Inn was the only retailer that had a direct account with Ganong Brothers of New Brunswick, makers of fine chocolates. (Pierre Ellyson)

I remember before the war when the Cherry Blossom chocolate bar was much bigger. It used to have a layer of dark chocolate first and then milk chocolate, and it cost only a nickel. (Charles W.K. Fraser)

I remember "working" at the Dew Drop in the 1960s as a kid, when my family stayed with Ken and Susie. One of my jobs was to "clean" the chocolates that were in the big display case. Ken would tell me to wipe down the chocolates. (Apparently as they got old they'd turn white, and Ken wanted them wiped off so that they'd look good for sale.) (Malcolm "Mac" MacLeod)

Perhaps the reason that the Dew Drop Inn offered such an amazing selection of sweet treats was that Ken had candy in his genes. Many years earlier, his cousins Jim and Jed Frasier had operated a candy factory in Cookshire.

Frasiers Candy Factory sign (Courtesy of Kerri Fraser)

Chapter 4   All kinds of goods

One experiences a few things in life for which words seem inadequate to properly describe. For me, the Dew Drop Inn store is one of them. Upon entering the place, your eyes beheld a smorgasbord of interesting stuff from floor to ceiling in every direction. Were it not for Ken's cheery "Hello," it was almost impossible to notice him standing there behind the cluttered counter. In fact, the scene reminds you of those "Where's Waldo?" puzzles. Your eyes vainly search for a focus but there is none. More accurately, there are too many focal points because the Dew Drop Inn store was really many stores intermingled within a single space. It was simultaneously a restaurant, a candy store, an ice cream parlour, a gift shop, a newsstand, a bookstore, a tobacco shop, a card shop, a paper shop, a community bulletin board, a cribbage den, a news central, a picture gallery, a private museum and a hangout for local anglophones. No wonder there was so much to see!

Ken Fraser behind Dew Drop Inn's counter (Fraser family archives)

This chapter will describe a few of the Dew Drop Inn's many component mini-shops. But first, some recollections of the store in general and of Ken, its keeper:

The storekeeper

Mr. Fraser was a merchant in the full sense of the word. It was clear that he liked to sell. In his soul, he was a convenience store manager before his time. His store had everything. You could feel his passion. As a francophone, one didn't feel especially at home there where everything reflected a world that largely eluded us. (Jean-François Nadeau)

He looked like the stereotypical shopkeeper with his glasses held with a chain and sitting on the tip of his pointy nose. (Charles C. Fraser)

Uncle Ken stood behind the curved wooden counter, always chatting. (Jim Fraser)

Uncle Ken was almost always behind the counter, often on his stool, near the wooden pull-out cash drawer. (Steve Fraser)

It was usually Uncle Ken who appeared at the counter immediately after the bell tinkled to announce that the front door had opened. I was always amused by the notices that Uncle Ken placed on his front door when he was not available for business. The sign said, "Closed, back in 5 (or 10 or 15 as the case may be) minutes." On Sundays the sign would read "Closed. At Church, you should be there too." (Marilyn Fraser Reed)

Ken had no love for the local IGA store. He called it the "I Grab All" store. (Bobbie Bowen)

What I best remember about Mr. Fraser was his distaste for the local IGA supermarket. When we asked him for something that he did not have in the store, he said, "Just go down the street to the IGA. IGA stands for 'I Got

Ken at Dew Drop Inn front entrance (P.Gualtieri photo)

it All', you know." He said that with a bit of sarcasm in his voice. (Rev. John Thevenot)

The store

To say that the Dew Drop Inn store was unique would be a huge understatement. From my first visit as a young child to my last visit more than 40 years later, I never ceased to be impressed with the volume and variety of its contents. I was fascinated by its peculiarities, such as the pull-out wooden cash drawer with the little round hemispheres for coins, and how Uncle Ken added up your bill on the side of a paper bag and then lopped off a 50 percent family discount.

In her article in the Globe and Mail of April 9, 1994, Jane George described Ken's "store-kingdom" as follows: "It was a store straight out of the past: wooden stairs, ceiling-high shelves, a tinny bell over the door and an owner who spun tales . . . No matter how many times I went to the Dew Drop Inn, I never could take full inventory of everything in the store."

Following is a summary of how others saw this venerable Cookshire institution.

> It had the feel of the past. It was jam-packed with all kinds of things – comics, candy, notions, etc. The diner booths were in front of the Main Street windows. Ken was always there, full of curiosity about anyone new to the area. (Muriel French Fitzsimmons)

> This unique place was, as it were, frozen in time. Electric trains, postcards of a bygone era – several of Cookshire including some of Dew Drop Inn itself. It was really a variety store. I remember that in the glass showcase there was a rare publication dating to about 1917 that told the story of the sons and daughters of Cookshire in World War I. There were also medals and coins bearing the heads of British monarchs. The store demonstrated an attachment to the British Empire. One sensed a Victorian flavour and a certain nostalgia with regard to the colonial past. (Jean-François Nadeau)

> The Inn itself was an extremely interesting place, mostly because of its furnishings. There was "old stuff" everywhere, and it was a real treasure trove for anyone who liked antiques or was nostalgic for those better days. (Rev. John Thevenot)

> The Dew Drop Inn was unique and truly special. All visitors and customers were mesmerized by the vast array of merchandise and interesting articles on display throughout the store, from floor to ceiling, literally. (Marilyn Fraser Reed)

> When you entered Dew Drop Inn, it seemed as if he had everything in this restaurant. I bought a mouth organ and a Jew's harp there, also a cribbage board that had belonged to Dr. Bennett. (Muriel Watson)

I remember most the millions of things for sale. When our kids were small, and we'd go to Cookshire on the weekend, one day our young daughter Dawn asked, "Are we going to stop at Uncle Ken's shopping center?" (June Fraser Patterson)

Mr. Fraser's Dew Drop Inn was a sort of capharnaum that simultaneously served as a café, gas station and the area's only taxi stand. (Jean-François Nadeau)

Ken behind the counter (P.Gualtieri photo, enhanced by G. Beck)

The place reminded me of another era, like something you see in American films. (Noël Landry)

It was like a historical relic that made you keep going back in for another visit to look around at all the interesting items on display. (Dorothy Shelton Dionne)

It brings me back to my childhood. I can't imagine any ride in the family car without seeing this building frozen in time. It was a landmark that reminded me that we were near home. The store had something about it that was at once disturbing and reassuring. Since its appearance hardly changed over the years, there was something mysterious about it. At the same time, the unchanging character of the place had the effect of situating Cookshire and its residents. There was a sort of sense of the period that the place itself silently expressed. (Jean-François Nadeau)

All kinds of goods

Dew Drop Inn, circa 1960; close-up of the sign (Photos by author)

The gift shop

Probably the most visually appealing part of the store was the large well-lit glass showcase cabinet that stood just on your right as you entered. It was impossible to miss, as your eyes were drawn to its very special contents. For us as kids, these items were expensive and untouchable. And only Uncle Ken could access them through the sliding doors at the back. As I came into my teenage years, I was able to afford something from this special case. It was film for my newly-acquired 35mm camera. And Uncle stocked only the best – Kodachrome II and Kodachrome 64 slide film that I continued to purchase on a regular basis for many years. Others share their own memories of this collectibles and curios cabinet:

> I bought my first pen knife from his showcase. I also remember the coin collection. (Charles C. Fraser)

He made his own souvenir items for tourists on which he painted "Cookshire" before displaying them in the showcase. (June Fraser Patterson)

I was always intrigued by the unique showcase with trains and other neat little things. I bought a salt and pepper shaker set with "Cookshire" painted on one and "Quebec" on the other. (Karen Fraser Jackson)

I remember most the showcase with the trains, coins, etc. (Christopher Standish)

I purchased my first watch from the display case. (Warren Fraser)

Souvenir mug from Dew Drop Inn (Courtesy of Marilyn Fraser Reed)

There was lots of stuff – some of dubious newness/ freshness. There were interesting items in the glass case, including a model train, coins, and Cookshire souvenirs (hand-lettered). Throughout the store were hand-lettered signs and notes. (Jim Fraser)

I still have the harmonica that he gave my son. (Louise Knox)

I remember the Lionel trains and all the other trinkets sequestered in the glass case. (Warren Fraser)

My best Christmas gift was the table hockey game that Dick and Marina gave to Winston and me in 1954 or 1955. I had been admiring it before Christmas as it sat on top of the chocolates showcase. (Malcolm "Mac" Fraser, from the Christmas 2001 issue of the Fraser Family Link)

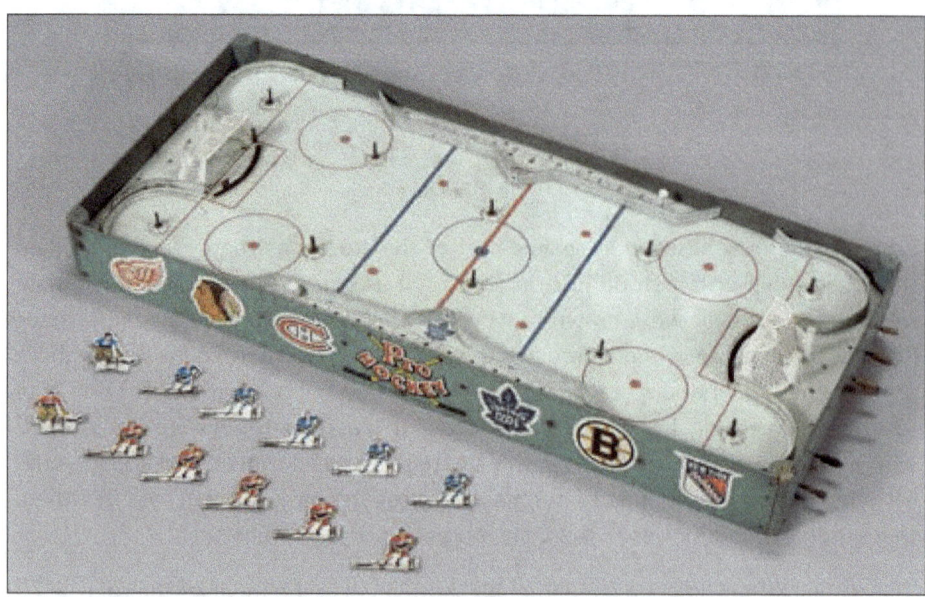

Table hockey game (www.historymusem.ca)

All kinds of goods

The newsstand

Dew Drop Inn carried almost every type of reading material known to man. From novels to newspapers. From comics to classics. From Railroad to Ring. From Patterns to Playboy. From National Geographic to National Enquirer. From Personal Finance to Personal Romance. Whatever your style, Ken had what you wanted. However, it wasn't always easy making the purchase of your preferred publication. For example, when my Aunt Winnie would go in to buy women's magazines such as "True Love" and "True Confessions," Uncle Ken would ask her, "What do you read these for?" or "Why on earth would you want to read that stuff?" Following are some other customers' newsstand experiences:

> In the heyday era of magazines, he undoubtedly offered the greatest selection in town. Many were the men who would go there to quietly purchase an erotic or slightly pornographic publication. I remember seeing Mr. Fraser reach under the counter to serve a hurried customer. (Jean-François Nadeau)

> I regularly purchased Hit Parade and similar magazines featuring the then-current musical heart throbs such as Paul Anka, Ricky Nelson and The Beatles. Often we were the recipients of free comic books with the titles cut off. (Marilyn Fraser Reed)

> There were dozens of "girly" magazines on display behind the counter. (David Fraser)

> Once, when I was probably six or seven years old, I bought a kind of Wonder Woman comic book. Nana was so furious about the perceived nudity that she stormed over to Ken's and asked him how he could sell something like that to a small child. Looking back it was quite funny. Nana was our grandmother, Hazel Burns. It was so convenient to visit the store when we were at her place next door. (Andrew Scott)

> We remember stopping there often when the children were young and buying the comic books with the top of the cover cut off for a very good price. (Doug and Eileen McGrory)

> There were two-cent comic books as well as five cent ones. (Warren Fraser)

> I remember the clutter of second hand novels, comics and magazines (including Playboy, which was a curiosity at the time). (Almon Pope)

> Ken would often provide unsold Superman and Batman comics to Warren and/or Steve. (Gloria Bellam)

> I remember choosing free comics with the tops cut off. (Charles C. Fraser)

In the restaurant behind the counter were lots of comics and magazines, many with their titles removed (cut off) that were quite a bit cheaper. (Eleanor Vogell Twyman)

I remember going in to buy comic books. The regular price was ten cents, but with the top cut off it cost only five cents. (Charlotte Taylor)

Ken sold a magazine, Rolling Stone, that I especially liked. He would usually have only a couple of copies. It was a monthly publication and a bit pricey, so Ken would just cut off the top portion of the cover and let me have one for free. He would do this with a lot of comic books as well. I think he got compensated when sending back the cut off portion, but I found this to be very kind of him. (Almon Pope)

I remember selecting various magazines like Sixteen and Teen for myself, but I would give my friend Doreen McDonald the money to pay for them so that Uncle Ken would not say to me, "You mean, you read that stuff?" I loved to browse through the old comic books that Uncle Ken would sell for five cents after the titles were clipped off. It was wonderful to be able to buy precious reading material for so little. We always read each other's comics, so if Steve or Warren bought some as well, we'd have plenty for several evenings' enjoyment. (Marilyn Fraser Reed)

After my marriage I would purchase the weekly TV Guide and the National Enquirer. Monthly it was Woman's Day and Family Circle. At times I would get a book or magazine on decorating. Ken had a good choice of magazines. I also purchased birthday cards, get well cards, etc. (Dorothy Shelton Dionne)

I remember reading cancelled comic books before Ken discarded them. He would clip the masthead of the front cover and return them for a refund. (Stan Parker)

I remember buying comic books. I also bought candy, books, and gas. (John Gill)

I was born and raised in Newport on Lawrence Road and attended elementary school in Island Brook and high school in Bury. My mother always bought her magazines at the Dew Drop Inn. (Norma Wiley)

Vintage Wonder Woman comic

All kinds of goods

I bought the Saturday Montreal Star there. (Steve Fraser)

Dad would buy all his magazines and comic books at Sherbooke News from a Mr. Gagnon. Dad would go there to pick them up. He was customer number 66. So sometimes as a kid, I'd go into the back room to look for the stack labelled "66" and bring it out to where Dad and Mr. Gagnon were talking. (Charles W.K. Fraser)

The tobacco shop

Knowing that Uncle Ken was strongly set against smoking, I always found it strange that he would sell cigarettes. Perhaps it is similar to the situation at that time where pharmacies sold cigarettes even though their prime mission is to treat illness and promote wellness. Unfortunately, it seems to boil down to the fact that "business is business." Nevertheless, our uncle must be given credit for being significantly ahead of his time in recognizing the dangers of smoking. Others share their memories of this aspect of the Dew Drop Inn's business below:

Besides cigarettes, Dad sold pipes and other smoking accessories. (Charles W.K. Fraser)

I was always amused but puzzled at first by Uncle Ken's lectures on the dangers of cigarettes. He displayed signs describing the dangers of smoking, targeted to those who were actually buying the cigarettes from him. (Marilyn Fraser Reed)

Uncle Ken had a prominent sign noting "The Five Big Cs of Smoking: Cigarettes, Cough, Choke, Cancer, Croak." (Jim Fraser)

Uncle Ken called cigarettes "cancer sticks" and "coffin nails." (Steve Fraser)

The card shop

The Dew Drop Inn greeting card display was one of the finest I have ever seen anywhere. It even rivalled the best of Hallmark's downtown card shops today. The cards were obviously carefully hand-picked as both the fronts and the inside verses were beautiful. The selection included both English and French cards. As with many of my siblings, I was often delegated to purchase cards for Mom and Dad to give each other for their birthdays, wedding anniversary, etc. Others share their greeting card experiences:

In 1956 when I moved to Montreal and worked as a photographer for the T. Eaton Company, I still came home on weekends and spent most of my time at Ken's. At the end of the Christmas season, Eaton's had a sale on Carlton and Coutts Christmas cards. We made a deal and Ken put up the money to buy their surplus stock. Ken sold in Cookshire through the Dew Drop Inn and I went door-to-door in Learned Plain, Island Brook,

Birchton and the surrounding countryside. We were selling boxes at 50 percent off and Ken sold individual cards at 25 percent off. But I had bought them all at 90 percent discount. That year, 1957, I made over $1,000 selling cards door-to-door. Ken and I always had a strong relationship. I didn't work at the Dew Drop Inn per se but if I was ever there and someone came in, I went behind the counter just to help out. (Rodger Heatherington)

I purchased cards for Dad to give to "Allie" for birthdays, etc. (Warren Fraser)

I remember buying, on Dad's behalf, greeting cards for Mom on all special occasions. (Jim Fraser)

Dew Drop Inn greeting card bag (Courtesy of Warren Fraser)

Mostly I purchased greeting cards requested by Dad, but sometimes by Mom also. (David Fraser)

I often bought birthday cards at the Dew Drop Inn. (Noël Landry)

Left: Greeting cards bought at Dew Drop Inn – front, inside verse (Fraser family archives)

Above: Ken's sign advertising French wedding cards (Fraser family archives)

Ken's sign advertising Valentine cards and chocolates (Fraser family archives)

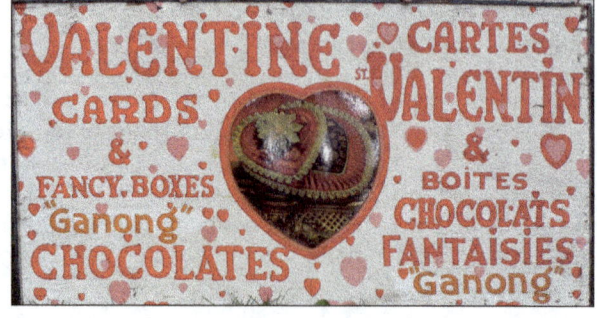

All kinds of goods

Odds and ends

There was practically no end to the kinds of items that one could buy at the Dew Drop Inn store. Recollections of a few miscellaneous purchases are shared below.

Black Cat firecrackers
(www.pinterest.com)

We purchased school supplies – pencils, notebooks (called scribblers way back then), etc. One day my friend, Jean Dunn, went in to buy a scribbler. Uncle Ken said, "That will be eight cents." Jean replied, "That is too much – at Osgood's store, it's only five cents." Says Uncle Ken, "Well, little girl, you just march right over to Osgood's store and get one." Says Jean, "But they don't have any left today." Says Uncle, "Well, when I don't have any left, they'll cost only three cents!" (June Fraser Patterson)

I remember that, money not being too available back then, Ken would allow many of us girls to buy Prismacolor pencil crayons one at a time. I don't think many other places would have allowed that then, and certainly not now! (Eleanor Vogell Twyman)

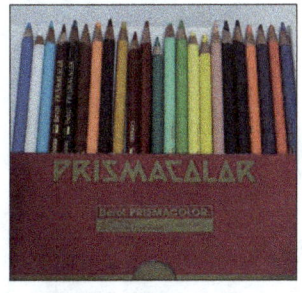

Vintage Prismacolor pencil crayons
(www.pinterest.com)

Mr. Fraser sold firecrackers when they were impossible to find anywhere else. I suspect that they came from the U.S.A. but I don't know how. He sold the Black Cat brand. And he sold other such items that were popular with teenagers. (Jean-François Nadeau)

I bought my firecrackers from Ken (always with cautionary advice). Once there was a grassfire attributed to them (not by anyone I know). As a result, I think they became an issue for Ken. So he stopped selling them to anyone with the exception of a few people (me being one), but that soon ended as well. We then bicycled to Island Brook and bought them from Earl Crawford's store. (Almon Pope)

I also purchased candy, comics, soft drinks, ice cream, ice cream bars, newspapers, cards, magazines and gifts. (Christopher Standish)

I remember seeing the "Closed for 5 minutes" sign on the front door of Dew Drop Inn, knowing full well that Uncle Ken was somewhere up in the Colony with his Hudson taxi picking up school students, and that it would be quite a few "5 minutes" before he would be back! (John "Jack" Fraser)

Dew Drop Inn

I remember the signs in the front window when the store was closed such as "Closed for 5 minutes" or "Gone to Church, hope to see you there too," etc. (Steve Fraser)

How could I ever forget the longest five minutes of my life, waiting on the front steps for Uncle Ken to return? (David Fraser)

I remember the various signs that Ken would put in the window when he was away from the store, such as "Gone for an hour," "Working in the garden," "On trip to Angus," etc. My sister Charlotte remembers his famous "Back in 5 minutes." (Bob Taylor)

A long 5 minutes (Sketch by James Harvey)

All kinds of goods

Shortly after Dad started the Dew Drop Inn business, he procured some kind of a pinball machine that was very illegal in those days. When it was discovered by the police, he had to go to court in Sherbrooke and ended up losing the machine. (Charles W.K. Fraser)

Ken bought many of the items for sale at Dew Drop Inn during regular trips to the U.S.A. to visit relatives. On one such occasion when he travelled by bus for a shopping spree in Springfield, N.H., he lost track of time and missed his return bus! This incident was documented in daughter Mabel's diary:

April 1, 1959: Shopped all day again. Folks out without coats or even sweaters. At 9:30 Dad phoned from Springfield to say that he'd missed the bus, and would be up on the bus that leaves there at 6 a.m. *(Ken had been shopping all day for items to sell at Dew Drop Inn.)* (Mabel Fraser's diary)

In addition to the Dew Drop Inn store on Main Street, Ken for several years operated a mini-store at the fairgrounds during the annual Cookshire Fair, where he sold various small items, chocolate bars, etc. He also was a Fair sponsor for many years by buying an ad in the Fair book. According to Jean Murray Chute's article in the Brome County News of November 2, 1994, Ken and Susie also provided meals at the Cookshire Fair for some 25 years.

Dew Drop Inn advertisements in Cookshire Fair books, 1951 (top) and 1958 (Courtesy of Neil Burns)

Chapter 5 Signs and wonders

Ken Fraser was a man of many talents and interests. But his great skill as a letterer and sign painter was what I found most impressive of all. I would stand and watch him for hours as he calmly applied his unmatched expertise to vehicles, billboards and smaller signs of all types. And I am not alone in my admiration of his work, as shown by the comments of others who witnessed some of his wonders.

Ken lettering vehicle behind Dew Drop Inn (Fraser family archives)

Ken's son Charles describes how his dad got into sign painting:

> Well, first of all, he became a painter's painter. He painted rooms in offices, and things like that, when he was still living in Sherbrooke. One day he was painting the walls inside a certain building and was asked to paint the top portion of the wall a different colour. Or maybe they wanted a different coloured strip across the middle of the wall. Whatever it was, Dad did it perfectly – and all freehand. The person in

charge was so impressed and amazed that he hired Dad as a sign painter. This was even before he started the Dew Drop Inn. Dad honed his lettering skills by studying books on calligraphy. But he was always good at drawing. He drew for me as a kid and he'd first make just two or three lines on a sheet of paper. Then he would say, "Guess what we're going to make." I would guess whatever, and he'd respond "No, I'm not making that." Then he'd draw a few more lines. Dad just loved sketching.

Truck lettering

It was magnificent! He lettered trucks and painted signs for various sales and businesses as well. An art that was still common in the early part of the 20th century has been rendered obsolete by the arrival of neons as its successors. I'd love to have one of these signs! Today this type of hand lettering is coming back as something distinguished. (Jean-François Nadeau)

Ken's sign and truck lettering was perfect. (Ben Hodge)

Back then, there was none of the vinyl that you put on the trucks today. Now they put it on the computer and pop it out and then stick it on. Ken painted everything by hand and did a very, very good job. On one big sign that I remember, he painted a cow grazing in the pasture – all kinds of stuff like that. And I mean BIG – on the side of a truck! (Bobbie Bowen)

Ken painted many trucks for my father and uncle. His painting was very clear and precise. (Christopher Standish)

I remember him always painting something at the side of the house, either a truck or a sign. (Greg Fraser)

Being somewhat "creative" myself, what really impressed me was Uncle Ken's immense talent doing lettering on trucks and signs. I watched him lettering trucks at least a couple of times. I remember how concentrated he was, hardly looking away from his work when speaking to me. What I remember most was the precision and beauty of his work, with the "shading effect" that gave depth and style to the lettering. A true professional! (David Fraser)

I remember watching Ken painting logos on business vehicles. God, he had a steady hand! (Andrew Scott)

I remember him sitting (not sure if it was on a stool or a crate) and painting lettering on the sides of vehicles. (Neil Burns)

I saw him at work many times at the side of Dew Drop Inn, usually sitting on a box with a small paintbrush in his mouth while he painted the truck cab. (Steve Fraser)

Signs and wonders

I watched him lettering a truck door and was amazed at his seemingly effortless brush strokes. (Warren Fraser)

I often saw him painting and I remember how meticulous he was -- he had a real flair for that work. (Betty MacRae Wright)

Uncle Ken was often in the left-hand driveway, sitting on a stool, expertly painting a truck. I remember watching him paint Lister's milk truck and the lettering was so beautiful. Afterwards, he would take another colour to shade it or something. Oh my, and all freehand! (June Fraser Patterson)

He used to letter large trailer trucks before they had decals. I remember him painting one in East Angus. They built a staging for him to stand on. He had to do the painting at night when the trucks were not in use. (Charles W.K. Fraser)

I remember him painting a truck's doors. He would do the greyish white base and let it dry. Then he would bold it, let it dry again and then do the highlights. He was very meticulous and had an amazingly steady hand and obvious patience. His work was very good indeed. (Almon Pope)

Often people would bring in just the door of the truck after they disconnected the hinges. After Dad finished the lettering a few days later, they would return to pick up the door and put it back on the truck. (Charles W.K. Fraser)

Many times I watched Ken painting, truck lettering. He did a very professional job, equal to a well-known painter from Sherbrooke who did my Uncle Everett's truck. (Stan Parker)

He always drew the lettering first on paper the size it was to be so that it came out perfectly. Never a drop of paint was wasted. (Dorothy Ross)

I remember Dad, one time when he was going to paint Paul Vallée's new truck, remarking about the truck's owner: "That fool, he paid $35,000 for that truck." (Charles W.K. Fraser)

Sign painting

Reverend Fairbairn asked me if I would ask Uncle Ken to redo the sign outside St. Peter's Anglican Church in Sherbrooke. Uncle Ken did it, and did a fantastic job. I think it was around 1980. And I don't believe he charged anything for his work. For many years this sign was outside the church for all to see. (Diane Fraser Keet)

I remember his large Dew Drop Inn sign near Slab City that extolled his Main Street establishment. (Warren Fraser)

I remember watching Uncle Ken as he meticulously painted all sorts of signs. The Pine Hill Farm sign was his creation, as was the banner for the 100th anniversary of Cookshire School. He also painted innumerable

Ken painting on stilts (Sketch by James Harvey)

advertisements for local events. I have two, one announcing an upcoming oyster supper and another a turkey supper. He seemed to paint effortlessly, but with obvious concentration. (Marilyn Fraser Reed)

In the photo of me and my family at the Cookshire Fair livestock parade, the sign that I am carrying was painted by Mr. Fraser. It shows me and my second son, Charles, as well as my brother Jacques, my employee Pierre and my brother Jean-Marie. Also, I saw him paint the door of Mr. Pageau's truck. (Noël Landry)

Noël Landry "Ferme Limpide" sign at Cookshire Fair (Photo by author)

B. Hodge Percherons sign, Island Brook, Que. (Photo by author)

Cookshire High School Centennial Reunion sign (Photo by author)

Sign on Pine Hill Farm's Canada Centennial maple sugaring float, 1967 (Fraser family archives)

When I opened the plant in Ayer's Cliff in 1976 for Ewing Records, Ken did all of the outdoor signs, as he did again when I bought the company and it became Everest Equipment Inc. Some of his signs were still in use until last year when the company changed hands again. That's 40 years! Also, as long as my father ran an electrical business, one of Ken's signs was on our garage roof. My son now has the sign hanging in his home. (Rodger Heatherington)

Uncle Ken painted the big stone down below the pond, the mailbox at Pine Hill Farm, countless lumber and construction trucks, and many other signs and posters. I loved watching him paint, freehand, a big truck parked on the side of the Dew Drop Inn. I have an original poster advertising a St. Patrick's Day concert in Bulwer. (Jim Fraser)

Soon after I arrived in Cookshire, Ken said, "You know Ronnie, you need to have a shingle." I said, "No. . . do I really need one?" and he said, "You're going to have a shingle." I said, "I'm afraid I don't have one." He said, "What would you like on your shingle?" I said, "The name is Ronald and I suppose Reverend would go before it and West after it." He said, "'Reverend West', that's too formal." He said, "Why not Rev. Ron West?" And that's what he did. I still have it on my shelf here. It was a piece of maple about three inches wide by maybe eight inches long, very nicely done. Ken designed it and Donnie Standish carved it. (Rev. Ron West)

Oyster supper poster (Courtesy of Marilyn Fraser Reed)

Installing Pine Hill Farm sign, 1989 (Photo by author)

He painted the huge boulder at the bottom edge of the upper pond with "Pine Hill Farm" and included a pine tree. (Warren Fraser)

Ken's hand-painted in-house advertising signs and notices were everywhere, inside and out. (Almon Pope)

Above: Reflector sign (Photo by author)

Right: Turkey dinner poster (Courtesy of Marilyn Fraser Reed)

I was fascinated by his easiness of the jobs at hand and how grand the painting was. (Karen Fraser Jackson)

Mothers Day Special sign (Photo by author)

Offsite jobs

Much of Ken's lettering and painting was done away from Dew Drop Inn, as shown by the following entries from Mabel's diary. Sometimes he would work late into the evening and even into the wee hours of the next morning before returning home.

> April 10, 1959: Dad down at Joe's Garage painting a truck nearly all evening.

May 19, 1959: Dad down to paint truck at St. Cyr's, and I kept store open and he got home at 8:20.

May 25, 1959: Helped Ma with flower boxes on side verandah. Dad to Island Brook to paint.

September 5, 1959: Daddy and Uncle Mike back from Sherbrooke at 12:30. Waited on store all day. Dad painted at Wallace's plant all afternoon.

November 21, 1959: Dad painted signs till after 1:00 a.m.

Supplies

Dad liked One Shot paint that he bought in Sherbrooke at CIL adjacent to the news distributor. Sometimes he would buy it in the States. He used camel hair brushes that he also bought in the States. (Charles W.K. Fraser)

One Shot brand is an oil-based enamel that comes in 46 colors. They were one of several companies that manufactured what was often called bulletin colors and were made for

Pine Hill Farm mailbox (Photo by author)

Weathered rock at Pine Hill Farm (Photo by author)

Rev. Ron West shingle designed by Ken (Courtesy of Ron West)

Ken Fraser initials between bricks at Pine Hill Farm (Photo by Warren Fraser)

Compton County Museum sign, Eaton Corner (Photo by author)

1-Shot sign painter's lettering enamel (www.amazon.com)

painting signs on everything – buildings, vehicles, etc. This was before the advent of the vinyl lettering that started in the early 1980s. (Source:http://www.modelcarsmag.com/forums/topic/97135-sign-painters-one-shot-enamel/)

Encouraging the young

Ken was a strong supporter of the annual Cookshire Fair. For example, he designed and painted a special licence plate that he installed on his car to promote the fair.

Wedding invitation design by Ken Fraser (Fraser family archives)

Cookshire Fair promo licence plate (Courtesy of Kerri Fraser)

Signs and wonders

He also sponsored special prizes to encourage the young to develop their artistic talents. He funded a $2.00 (merchandise) sponsorship special prize for the "16 years and under" class as follows:

- 1951   Best Hobby
- 1958   Best Hobby
- 1960   Best Hobby
- 1962   Best Hobby
- 1963-1965   Best pencil or crayon drawing
- 1964   Best pencil or crayon Greeting Card
- 1965   Best pencil or crayon Greeting Card

Cookshire Fair, circa 1980 (Photo by author)

Dew Drop Inn

Chapter 6   In the upper room

Although the store was the most visible part of the Dew Drop Inn complex, it was by no means the only centre of business activity. Upstairs on the second floor was another beehive of commerce in the form of Susie's hairdressing salon, aptly named Suz-Ann Beauty Parlour. For most of its 50-plus years of operation it was located upstairs, though it was initially downstairs on the main level and returned there for its final years of operation.

Original sign for Suz-Ann Beauty Parlour (Photo by author; enhanced by G. Beck)

Evolution

Son Charles tells the story of how it all began.

> Mom started the beauty salon in 1936 and here is the reason why. My Dad wouldn't let Mom purchase some kind of insurance plan that would put away money for my sister Mabel's college education. My sister was

eight years old at the time. So Mom said "Well, that's fine. I'm going to start my own business." And so she did. Dad painted a large sign for her new business and hung it out front, just under the Dew Drop Inn sign. Mom named the shop Suz-Ann Beauty Parlor. To learn the trade, Dad would drive her down to East Angus where a Mrs. Campbell taught hairdressing. (Charles W.K. Fraser)

L-R: Mabel, Jack MacLeod, Charles, Susie; circa 1940 (Courtesy of Mac MacLeod)

Family and friends share their observations and impressions of Susie's beauty salon:

> First she had it in the shed behind the kitchen but there was no room back there. So they moved it upstairs and made it very nice. (Bobbie Bowen)

> It was upstairs, just at the top of the stairs. I might have gone up there to meet someone or to take something to Aunt Susie. (John "Jack" Fraser)

> The shampooing, cutting, shaping and all that was done upstairs in the room right at the head of the stairs. The dryer was in the next room. I think Mom only had one main dryer upstairs. She had a hand dryer or two, but only the one main heavy chair-mounted dryer there. But later when the salon moved back downstairs, I know she had at least two or maybe three dryers. (Charles W.K. Fraser)

In the upper room

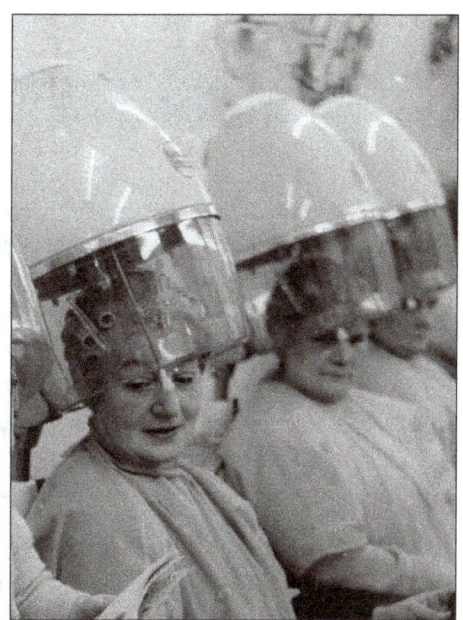

Left: 1930s vintage permanent machine (www.pinterest.com)
Right: 1930s vintage hair dryers (www.pinterest.com)

Suz-Ann Beauty Parlour calendar (www.ebay.com)

What I remember most about Susie's beauty salon was the smell of ammonia. (Rodger Heatherington)

I remember that Susie used a hair-setting gel called "Dippity-do" when doing women's hair. (Charlotte Taylor)

What I remember most was this thing with wires attached to it that she would pull down from the ceiling and place over the person's head to dry their hair. It was a horrible looking contraption and I was afraid that the person would get electrocuted! (Johnny Scholes)

After more than 20 years operating out of the upstairs location, Susie moved her salon downstairs. At the same time, she expanded and modernized. This milestone event was noted in Mabel's diary.

> October 31, 1959: . . . had my hair done in Ma's new shop, I was the first customer.

Clientele

Susie's customer base was large and loyal. Even though older women represented the majority of her clientele, she served young women as well. For example, at least two brides entrusted their wedding day hairdos to Susie – Joyce Standish in 1946 and daughter Mabel in 1960. No doubt there were others through the years. Below are recollections about some of the many women and girls who were made beautiful thanks to Susie's skills.

Dippity-do hair setting gel, 1960s (incurlers.blogspot.ca)

> Mrs. Pat (Marcel) Roy was an extremely loyal customer from Learned Plain. After she moved to Stanstead, she still came back to Cookshire to have Susie do her hair. (Rodger Heatherington)
>
> My mother (Estelle Frasier) and I would go there to get "perms." We had to go in the back door and up the stairs to reach the salon. There was only one chair. Susie also sold various beauty products. (Gloria Frasier Bellam)
>
> My grandmother, mother, and Aunt Joyce all went to Susie's beauty salon. (Christopher Standish)
>
> Every time we visited, she would cut my hair. There were always clients in the salon. (Greg Fraser)
>
> The parlour was always busy on Saturdays. We'd come and go through there while my grandmother was doing hair. (Kerri Fraser)
>
> Suzy did my hair for my wedding. (Joyce Standish)
>
> I had Suzy cut my hair and give me permanents. She always wore a white dress or some type of apron when doing her customers' hair. (Muriel Watson)
>
> Among Susie's clients were Ethel Woolley, Elizabeth Farnsworth, Esther Farnsworth and Henrietta Hodgman. (Dorothy Ross)
>
> I think most of the town ladies were customers of hers because they always seemed so well coiffed. Neighbouring towns' customers were also there regularly. I remember going upstairs and seeing the beauty parlor and I remember the pleasant smells of shampoos, etc. (June Fraser Patterson)

In the upper room

Ken and Mabel at Mabel's wedding, 1960 (Courtesy of Louise Knox)
Right: Joyce Standish at her wedding, 1946 (Courtesy of Joyce Standish)

I recall that Cousin Lena Joyce and Aunt Maude Patton were patrons of Aunt Susie's salon. (Jim Fraser)

My mother and I had our hair done by Susie. I remember that she once gave our Girls Auxiliary group a tour of her salon and demonstrated her hairdressing skills on Dr. Bennett's wife. (Betty MacRae Wright)

Susie had her hairdressing salon upstairs. I remember going there with my grandmother and mother when they had their hair done. I believe she sold some cosmetics, perfume, etc. there too. (Eleanor Vogell Twyman)

Yes, indeed I remember Susie's beauty salon and was a client on many occasions for a "permanent." I marvel today how we endured such things (and their smells and twisted results) for fashion, and how it was considered necessary for children. (Dr. Emily Hamilton)

When my hair would get long, Susie would say, "Oh, you come, Louise and I'll give you a trim." So, I'd go and sit in a chair and she'd cut my hair. (Louise Knox)

I remember that my mom and grandmother went to Susie to get their hair done. (Pat Stevenson Smith)

Various entries in Mabel's diary confirm that Susie's salon was a very busy place indeed. But, in spite of her busyness, she was able to find time to give herself a permanent!

January 10, 1959: Ma did my hair. Ma had person in afternoon and 3 customers after supper.

February 16, 1959: Busy. In evening I helped Ma give herself a permanent.

Against the law

Bailiff padlocks Suz-Ann Beauty Parlour (Sketch by James Harvey)

In the upper room

Susie was known to charge somewhat less than the going rate, especially in the case of seniors. Unfortunately, her benevolence got her into trouble with the law. Son Charles and nephew Jim provide the details.

> In the 1980s, someone made a complaint because Mom was undercharging seniors. The hairdressers union then came and padlocked the side verandah door and closed her down. As a result, she was forced to obtain her official certification. This involved studying and doing the exams in French. I am very proud of the fact that she did it and passed the exams! (Charles W.K. Fraser)

> Hairdressing was (and perhaps still is) a tightly regulated business in Quebec. Aunt Susie was in her 80s when she had to renew her licence and was proud that she successfully met the challenge from the Office de la langue française by passing her French language competency test. (Jim Fraser)

A team of one

The indefatigable Susie operated the hairdressing business entirely by herself. She had no receptionist, no hair washer, no janitor, no esthetician, no salesperson, no buyer – nobody but herself. Son Charles comments:

> Mom never had any helpers. But there was one time when she really should have had some help. She used to put large flower pots around the front gallery of Dew Drop Inn. One day she dropped one of them on her toe. Obviously she wasn't in very good shape for getting around. So she had me attach wheels to a chair. That way, she could kneel on the chair to move among her customers.

Susie continued her hairdressing right up until it was time to close the Dew Drop Inn following Ken's passing. Closing the business after so many years was obviously not easy for her. She expressed her sadness in a 2000 interview with The Record: "My, I hated to leave my customers. That was very difficult, and then leaving my old home was worse."

Ken and Susie in front of Dew Drop Inn, 1988 (Photo by Almon Pope)

Dew Drop Inn

Chapter 7   Ride in his chariot

Yet another facet of Dew Drop Inn's impressive variety of business ventures was Ken's taxi service. But before looking at this aspect in more detail, it behooves us to mention his fascination with automobiles in general and classic models in particular. Later in this chapter we will look at Ken's gas station business.

Taxi driver Ken in front of Dew Drop Inn,
circa 1938 (Fraser family archives)

Ken's cars

Ken's great interest in the motor vehicle was passed on to his son Charles, who remembers the details of every single car that his dad ever owned.

> Dad's very first car was a Model-T Ford. It was before they had a starter, so it would have been pre-1915, probably a 1912 or 1914 model. Then he had another Model-T that did have an electric starter. However, Hibbert Sargent had fixed the first Model-T spark to be able to start it by itself by moving the spark advance in a certain direction. And the first Model-T would start more often by wiggling this modified control than the newer model with the factory-installed electric starter!

Top: Ken's first car was a 1914 Model T Ford (www.insideevs.com)
Above: Ken's last car was a 1951 Hudson Hornet (www.pinterest.com)

Next he had a 1929 Plymouth. The neat thing about it was it had a curtain that could be pulled up or down over the rear window. Then he had a 1937 Buick. It had a nice 8-cylinder – a nice straight-eight.

During the war, when parts were hard to get, Mr. Nourse (who had a garage behind the post office) said that all the bearings were gone on the rear end of the Buick. He told Dad that the Ford bearings would fit and Dad said, "Oh my God, are you sure?" He said he was 100 percent certain that it would last longer than the original New Departure bearings. So, the Buick ended up with Ford bearings in the differential. At least twice I was with Dad when the rear axle broke on that Buick. Again Mr. Nourse found that the Chevy axles would fit the Buick and they were bigger and stronger.

Next he had the 1947 Hudson that he bought in Belleville, Ont. from Bill DeLion and Borden Gill. Borden had come down that spring with a beautiful gray Hudson. But Dad said "No, I can't afford that." Soon afterwards, we just happened to take a trip down to the New England states and the old Buick broke down four times on the way to Montpelier, Vermont. My Uncle Fred McCormick told Dad that he couldn't drive that car much longer. So he took it to a garage that Uncle Fred used down there and left it to be repaired. Uncle Fred lent him his '47 Hudson Coupe. When we got back home, Dad decided to change cars. That first Hudson went about 400,000 miles. The next Hudson, this one brand new, was a 1950 Pacemaker followed by a 1951 Hudson Wasp. My sister had the '47 Hudson for a few years, then she had the chance to get a '51 Hornet. Dad took over the Hornet after Sister passed. That was his last car and the one that so many people remember.

Ken had great difficulty parting with his old cars when he would buy newer models. They would often end up in the garage behind the Dew Drop Inn and remain there indefinitely. When he overflowed his garage's capacity, he would sometimes offload a vehicle or two to my dad's farm, where they would stay for years. Dad would keep bugging Uncle Ken for years to remove the "car-casses." Finally he took them away for scrap, but by then trees had grown up through them. My brother David remembers one of these parked vehicles and my Mom's diary records some additional details of their fate:

> One of Uncle Ken's old Hudsons that he used for parts was parked beside the Pine Hill Farm toolshed for several years. I used to like getting behind the wheel and taking it for an imaginary drive around the countryside (since we were never allowed to get behind the wheel of the farm tractor). (David Fraser)
>
> November 1, 1959: Call from Kenneth getting car. (Alice Fraser's diary)
>
> October 22, 1963: Call from Kenneth getting pieces from old car. (Alice Fraser's diary)

Various folks, young and old, particularly remember Ken's classic Hudson cars.

> What young impressionable boy could forget his Hudson car? (Neil Burns)
>
> My grandfather talked about Mr. Fraser's Hudson, and I remember seeing the car in the garage. (Jean-François Nadeau)
>
> I remember Ken's "Hudson Hornet" cars. (Charlie Twyman)

Public taxi

Ken provided two flavours of taxi service – a paid service for the general public and an unpaid service for family. And, according to a sign in the upper right hand window of Dew Drop Inn that read "TAXI – DAY and NIGHT," he offered his taxi services on a 24-hour-a-day, 7-day-a-week basis. Son Charles relates how his dad first got into the taxi business:

> It was a question of necessity. Dad had to become an officially registered taxi because he was already taxiing people around on an informal basis. If he continued, he was going to be pinched by the authorities. He stayed in the taxi business for many years until the cops used to stop him every second time that he took his Hudson out on a taxi run. The police said the car was unsafe and they used to take him up to Neilson's Garage in Eaton Corner. When they'd get there, Nielsen would tell the cops "This car is safer than the one you are driving!" You see, the old Hudsons had double brakes underneath the foot pedal -- if the hydraulic brake failed, the mechanical brake automatically caught in and took over.
>
> In terms of the rates that my dad charged, I remember that the fare to

Sherbrooke was $2 and if he had to wait he'd suggest that the customer give him $2.25.

Following are some memories of people who used Ken's taxi service:

When I was going to school in Cookshire and went home to Island Brook, Ken often had trips to Island Brook, and I would get a ride back to Cookshire with him on Sunday. (Muriel Watson)

When I could afford it I hired Ken to take me home to Island Brook on Friday nights after school. He always kept me up on all the news and also told his stories. (Dorothy Ross)

Part of our C.H.S. hockey team used his taxi services on occasion. I think this happened when our senior team and peewee/intermediate team had games at the same time and Frank Woolley's bus would be overfull. I remember hearing a story about a Scotstown trip when part of the team showed up late – not sure whether Ken had a breakdown or what happened. (Almon Pope)

Ken once drove me to Pep's in Lennoxville to meet Don after our daughter Trish had broken her leg at Quebec Lodge camp. He was very generous – I remember that he refused payment for this trip. (Joyce Standish)

I remember going along for the ride in the Hudson on trips to Sherbrooke, East Angus and all around the countryside. (Bobbie Bowen)

During the war, when she did not have a car, my mother Estelle Frasier would have Ken pick her up to go to Susie's to have her hair done. (Gloria Bellam)

Neither Rev. Turpin nor Rev. Grey had cars, so Dad used to taxi them around to various places. (Charles W.K. Fraser)

Several different travelling salesmen would come on the train with their big suitcases. Dad would pick them up at the station and take them on their rounds to Lime Ridge, Sawyerville, etc. and even up to Randboro to service the various little country stores. (Charles W.K. Fraser)

I remember being driven by Ken to Bishop's University after a visit to my grandfather in Cookshire. (Barbara Challies)

Ken drove me to Sherbrooke Hospital in January 1953 prior to my giving birth to Liles. (Gloria Bellam)

My sisters and I would use Ken's taxi service to go to the movie theatre in East Angus on occasion. Susie would always come along for the ride and sit in the front. (Doris Pope)

In the fifth grade, I attended a convention in Montreal as a Red Cross representative with a few other students (including either Malcolm or John) via Ken's Hudson taxi. When we stopped outside the Sun Life

Building on Dorchester Square, Ken said to us, "Now, when you get out of the car, don't look up, because if you do, then everybody will know that you're from the country." Naturally, we all looked up! (David Mackay, from the January 2016 issue of the Fraser Family Link)

May 6, 1950: Marina & John went to MTL for Red Cross meeting with other school kids & Kenneth took them, left here at 5:15 AM returned 9 PM. (Alice Fraser's diary)

Montreal in the 1940s, showing the prominent Sun Life Building (Postcard from author's collection)

I too remember going on an elementary school trip to Montreal in Uncle Ken's taxi to see the Sun Life building. I still remember those huge tubs of Hunting's ice-cream that dear Uncle brought along.

May 28, 1955: Winston went to MTL with Ken & school kids. Returned 9:15 PM. (Alice Fraser's diary)

Ken took a bunch of students to Montreal on a Red Cross rally for a school trip. He found a park for us to eat our lunch at noon hour. (Dorothy Shelton Dionne)

On Sunday, January 10, 1940, my mother played the organ and sang in the choir at Cookshire United Church. After Church, she called Ken to take her to Montreal. Ken inquired if she was going to visit family. She said "No" and explained that he was to take her to the hospital in Montreal – where I was born the following day! No one at Church or at home, including my father, was aware that she was even pregnant. Ken was the first to know and called my father with the news. (Rodger Heatherington)

In later years when I worked at Ken's part-time, I remember that he didn't like doing long trips. There was a Mrs. Bailey who lived in the Wootten apartments who had to go to the hospital in Montreal, but he didn't like to do such trips. The fee at that time was $100." (Rodger Heatherington)

Ken's Hudson taxi-school bus (Sketch by James Harvey)

Ride in his chariot

One day, Dad took Dr. Bennett up to a patient near North River somewhere. When the doctor came out of the house, Dad asked him, "How did it go?" Dr. Bennett said, "Oh, pretty good." Later in the conversation, Dr. Bennett told him that the patient's previous doctor had charged an exorbitant amount. So when the patient asked, "How much is it, Doctor?" he replied "Nothing." So Dad didn't charge Dr. Bennett anything either! (Charles W.K. Fraser)

The Roy family used Ken and his Hudson as a school bus from Learned Plain. (Christopher Standish)

Ken drove us students from the Cookshire school to the Sawyerville school for Grade 10, and then brought us back at noon. At exam time we used to go over to the Dew Drop Inn and sit in the restaurant to wait between exams. (Alberta Everett)

He used to ferry schoolkids to/from The Colony and Learned Plain. (Charles W.K. Fraser)

He drove Hazel McVetty to and from her work at Frasier, Thornton and Co., and often picked up parcels for us at the station, as my father ran the meat market. (Betty MacRae Wright)

Cookshire taxi licence plate, 1960 (Photo by Greg Fraser)

I accompanied him occasionally on some of his taxi runs. That's why I treasure his taxi license plate from 1960 – the year I was born. (Greg Fraser)

I remember a hilariously funny story about Ken and his taxi when I was visiting one winter. Way back in the 1950s, in the wintertime, his taxi's windshield would ice up on the inside when it got extremely cold. To fix the problem, Ken put a little bit of alcohol on a rag that he wrapped up together with a single-edge razor blade. He would keep it on the dashboard with a rubber band around it. When the window would ice up, he would use the device and almost instantly, the ice was gone. A travelling salesman taxi customer sitting in the back seat says, "What have you got in that thing that took the ice off so fast?" Ken replies "Oh that's Jeezlum-side-borax" and the guy says "It's what?" Ken repeats "It's Jeezlum-side-borax." The guy asks "Well, where can I get that?" Ken tells him "In hardware stores; they probably have it behind the counter." Well, about a month or two goes by and this same travelling salesman shows up again. Ken telephones me in New York and says, "You've got to hear what happened." I said, "What happened?" and Ken says, "Remember the salesman that you were with in the car that day, when the windows were all frosted up?" And I said, "Yeah?" and Ken says, "He told me that he had gone to every hardware store in his area looking for "Jeezlum-side-borax" but he couldn't find it anywhere!" (Bobbie Bowen)

Ken and Susie with Charles and Jack MacLeod in front of Dew Drop Inn (Fraser family archives)

Former Anglican Church in Lawrence Colony (Photo by author)

Family taxi

Because my dad never owned a car, our family had to count on others to go anywhere beyond walking distance. And more than nine times out of 10, it was Uncle Ken who took us there and brought us back. Whether it involved medical appointments, Church suppers or sports events, our dear uncle cheerily ferried us to and fro. And the price was right. As far as I know, neither my parents, my siblings nor myself ever paid as much as a penny for this taxi-on-demand service. My siblings well remember this service that our mom so well documented in her daily diary entries, excerpts of which are shown following their recollections:

Donald and Alice Fraser and their 12 children, circa 1955 (Fraser family archives)

> All of the Fraser clan were shuttled pro bono hither and yon by Uncle Ken. (Warren Fraser)

> Uncle Ken drove us to the dentist office in East Angus each summer. We joked that our uncle's Hudson moved too slowly. (Marilyn Fraser Reed)

Uncle Ken drove me and my siblings to the Cookshire Fair and to Bury on the first of July. He also drove us to dentist appointments in East Angus. Although I don't actually remember it, he probably drove me to hospital when I had a ruptured appendix. (Karen Fraser Jackson)

He would go to the station to pick up relatives coming to visit and deliver them back. He would pick up the doctor and/or midwife for the births of most of the Fraser 12 siblings. (John "Jack" Fraser)

We the Frasers used his taxi service from time to time, but I don't recall anyone ever paying him for this service – but Mom must have. Some rides that I recall: taking veggies and maple products to and from Cookshire Fair; going to see the fireworks in Bury on July 1 (from a small hill far away from Bury); and being transported to Sherbrooke Hospital with appendicitis when I was five years old. (Jim Fraser)

June 6, 1952: Marina babysitting at Rev's. Kenneth brought Marina home at 10 PM & stayed till 12:30.

Dec. 4, 1954: In evening Dad & Ma went to oyster supper in Birchton, went up on bus, back with Ken.

Feb. 20, 1956: Ken in AM taking things to Seed Fair.

Aug. 19, 1956: Ken took Dad & boys to fair with things in AM.

Feb. 15, 1957: Ken took Dad & Ma to Dr Klinck's (for) nose bleeds, thence to Hospital.

July 15, 1960: David got nail in foot. Ken took he & I to Dr Lepine.

June 12, 1962: Ken took Jimmy & Ma to hospital. Little Jimmy had appendix operation at 2:10 AM. Ken brought Ma home at noon.

Aug. 19, 1964: Uncle took Mom & kids to H. & Y. dentist in East Angus. (Explanatory note re "H. & Y.": We had gone to old Dr. Veilleux for a few years and when he retired or died, his son (I believe) took over. However, he was not only H.andsome & Y.oung but also very expensive so we went to him only that one time!)

Nov. 8, 1965: Uncle took us to vote.

Gas pumps

The pair of brightly coloured Shell gas pumps was, for almost half a century, a prominent feature in front of the Dew Drop Inn. In fact, Ken was a Shell dealer for more than 40 years. One of the walls inside the Dew Drop Inn displayed the many Shell long-service award plaques he accumulated over that time.

I worked once at the Dew Drop Inn pumping gas. I was petrified because I had no idea where to find the gas cap because for different cars it was in different places.

Friends beside gas pump and oil bottles, circa 1940 (Courtesy of Bobbie Bowen)

Mabel and Charles beside gas pump, circa 1945 (Courtesy of Mac MacLeod)

And I really panicked if someone asked me to check their oil. How would I open the hood and where would I find the oil stick? Believe me, I was totally non-automotive!

Following are others' memories of the Dew Drop Inn gas station:

> Dad sold McColl Frontenac gas and oil products for a few years before he became a Shell distributor. (Charles W.K. Fraser)

> My earliest memories were when I started school at five years old. I knew I was almost there at school when I saw Uncle Ken's gas pumps. (June Fraser Patterson)

> I recall the old vertical gas tanks which I believe disappeared sometime during the following decade. (Dr. Emily Hamilton)

> I remember watching cousin Charles pump gas and telling him how easy his chores were compared to ours on the farm. He thought otherwise! (June Fraser Patterson)

> I remember selling gas at 42 cents a gallon! (Malcolm "Mac" Fraser, from the Christmas 1994 issue of the Fraser Family Link)

> I remember Ken pumping gas and checking under the hoods. (Andrew Scott)

Ken's Shell 30-year service award plaque (Photo by Greg Fraser)

Running a gas station was not without its challenges. During the late 1960s or the early 1970s there was some sort of strike of petroleum retailers in Quebec. Distributors were not allowed to sell gas, but Uncle Ken said, "To hell with them, I'm selling gas." Before long, a bunch of goons arrived at the Dew Drop Inn. Charles remembers: "I was there and it scared the dickens out of me. I would say that there were three or four burly fellows who came. I was scared for my dad." Uncle Ken had no other choice but to close for the duration of the strike. Then, a few years later, he had to close down his gas pumps forever due to strict environmental regulations that had been legislated. This latter incident was not his only negative experience with the Quebec government. Some years earlier, it was determined that the large unilingual Dew Drop Inn sign that hung on the front of the store contravened the government's language laws. He solved the problem by painting over the offending words but retaining those that were spelled the same in French as in English!

Above: Ken with sign beside closed gas pumps, circa 1975 (Fraser family archives)

Right: "Whitewashed" Dew Drop Inn signs, 1978 (Photo by Jim Fraser)

License to sell gasoline, 1931 (Photo courtesy of Charles W. K. Fraser)

Chapter 8   From evening till morning

The Dew Drop Inn had no fixed closing time. Even if the main door with the little tinkle bell was locked, one could usually gain access via the side verandah door. Most likely Ken or Susie would be in the kitchen busily working at something. I would dare speculate that the lights never were shut off completely – which must have been good for Southern Canada Power, the company that provided electricity back then. Without a hint of exaggeration, there was something happening there almost 24 hours a day. In this chapter, we look at some of Dew Drop Inn's after-hours activities.

"The One That Got Away" (Cookshire postcard from author's collection)

Playing cards

Without a doubt, Cookshire's Dew Drop Inn was the cribbage capital of the Eastern Townships and perhaps of the entire country! Many recall this activity that sometimes lasted late into the night.

> Don used to play cribbage with Ken and several others. (Joyce Standish)

> My daughter, Randi, often used to play crib with Ken after school while waiting for her bus. (Rodger Heatherington)

Card hand (www.the-room-mom.com) and cribbage board (www.zontikgames.com)

I remember Rev. Vallis in particular. He would drop by the Dew Drop Inn and visit or play cribbage. He smoked and I remember that he was known to have a drink on occasion. I think he may have got ribbed a bit on his vices although Ken seemed to like him. (Almon Pope)

I played crib with Ken at the store. He was a great crib player. (Christopher Standish)

I played cribbage with Uncle Ken. I don't remember but I can pretty well guess that he probably skunked me. I remember thinking how very fast he could count his hands. (Karen Fraser Jackson)

I used to play cribbage with Uncle Ken every now and then and basically, he could know the card Susie played before she put the hand down. He could tell her what she had in her hand. I don't know how he had done it but he did. It was his memory. (Rev. Ron West)

I played crib every Friday, Saturday and Sunday evening with Uncle Ken, Donnie Standish and Darrell Bellam. (Malcolm "Mac" Fraser, from the Christmas 1994 issue of the Fraser Family Link)

I remember playing cribbage with Uncle Ken only once or twice. The fact that he could glance at a hand and know how many points it was worth, without counting everything out, fascinated me. He'd laugh at my feeble attempts at cribbage math! (Jim Fraser)

I remember sitting in the adjoining booth at the Dew Drop Inn as Ken, Darrell Bellam, Donnie Standish and I think Claude Drennan or Cecil Gilbert played cribbage every week on a certain night. It was very entertaining for us young guys. The language could be quite flamboyant. Donnie or Ken would emulate passing gas with their lips each and every time. And I remember Donnie's standard count of "15:2, 15:4 and there's a whore at the door." They had a variety of other choice counts. (Almon Pope)

That's how I learned to count, by playing cribbage. (Charles W.K. Fraser)

From evening till morning

> April 26, 1959: Johnston came in the evening. Men played crib. (Mabel Fraser's diary)

> Darrell was a frequent cribbage player at Dew Drop Inn. (Gloria Bellam)

Sometimes, cribbage seemed to get in the way of business as illustrated in the incident recounted below.

> I remember one time when Mr. Fraser and his friend Mr. Jackson were playing crib when a stranger walks in, examines some of the toy trains and asks if they are for sale. The answer from Ken: "Maybe." (Pierre Ellyson)

But cribbage wasn't the only card game that occupied their evenings. Ken and Susie frequently attended card parties in the surrounding area such as Bulwer, Sand Hill, Moe's River, etc. Apparently they played very well as a team and often came away as winners. In fact they won so often that it became problematic. Son Charles explains.

> Mom and Dad were great card players. Because they won so many years in the 500 group, they were told that they couldn't play in that group any longer but instead they would have to join the bridge group. So they played bridge the next year, and won again! They made a great pair because however Mom would bid, Dad could read exactly what she had in her hand and know what he should do. (Charles W.K. Fraser)

> Although I never played cards with them, I do know that they went everywhere where there was a card party happening. (Dorothy Ross)

Bulwer Community Centre (Photo by author)

Visiting

Being the gathering place that the Dew Drop Inn was, it is not surprising that friends would come and go at all hours of the day or night to visit or just hang out. Mabel's diaries record friends' visits that sometimes lasted almost until sunrise.

> February 6, 1959: . . . Shortly after midnight Rodger landed back from Angus. Left his car there and walked as far as Farnsworth's. Hugh in after 2. Boys stayed till nearly 3:30.
>
> September 12, 1959: To bed at 1:30 a.m. and up at 2:30 to let the boys in. Then Rodger, Barb and Sliver arrived – then Ronnie. Gang left and went to bed at 3:30. A.M. Les then drove San home at 4, when he and Bob came to bed.

Everyone who knew Ken was aware of how much he enjoyed visiting, whether at the Dew Drop or elsewhere. One of his favourite places to visit was Pine Hill Farm. He called it simply "the farm." It was, after all, where he was born and grew up. He came quite frequently and often stayed for hours. He particularly enjoyed springtime visits to the maple sugar bush where he would often leave inscriptions on the walls of the sugar camp. My mom's diary documents his many visits and some of my siblings share their memories of them following:

January 14, 1954: (10 min) visit from Kenneth in eve. *("10 min." was underlined in the diary, indicating that this was an unusually short visit for him!)*

April 2, 1957: Dad & John finished boiling, Ken went up *(to the sugar camp)*

November 23, 1959: Uncle Ken in eve for 10 minutes, staying 2 hours

January 3, 1974: Uncle Ken for 2 1/2 hrs playing cards.

I remember Uncle Ken visiting the farm even before my first introduction to the Dew Drop Inn. It was always entertaining to listen to him as he stood in the kitchen at the front door with his hand on the knob and saying "I

Ken and Susie at 1993 Fraser Family Reunion (Photo by author)

must leave now." Fifteen minutes later he was still chatting. We loved it. (Marilyn Fraser Reed)

When Uncle Ken would come to visit Grammy, and we were upstairs in bed, we tried to listen to his stories because he used such colourful and forbidden vocabulary! (June Fraser Patterson)

He often came to the farm, stood with his hand on the doorknob, ready to leave, and would stand there in that position for another 30 to 45 minutes telling stories. It was always fascinating to listen to him. We were glad he didn't rush out." (Diane Fraser Keet)

Pine Hill Farm sugar camp, circa 1960 (Photo by author)

Left: K. I. F. carving on sugar camp wall. 1934 (Photo by author)
Right: Ken's Expo '67 inscription on wall (Photo by author; enhanced by G. Beck)

Sugar camp inscription, 1953 (Photo by author)

Sports

Ken loved sports, especially skating, hockey and baseball. Many a winter evening he spent on the rink behind the school; in the summer he was at the ballpark down by the river. Besides participating in these sports, he was also an enthusiastic fan who followed the professional teams. I especially remember the Yankees-Dodgers World Series of the 1950s. We would go upstairs into the Dew Drop Inn's living room to watch the games on TV. He would get very excited and jump to his feet and curse Casey Stengel as the Yankees' manager emerged from the dugout to argue with the umpire.

Ken was very proud of the local Cookshire sports teams and had old photos of them displayed on the wall behind the Dew Drop Inn counter. One of the photos that he enjoyed showing was of the Cookshire town hockey taken around 1920. Another was of the 1961 C.H.S. champion track and field team.

Others share their memories of Ken's interest and involvement in sports. Mabel's diary mentions additional sports events and activities.

> Ken was a very good skater. Late in the evening, at skating times or after a hockey practice, he'd be out there skating even in the coldest weather. (Stan Parker)

> I remember Ken skating at the rink behind the school one Friday night. He had skates that were attached to his boots. (Christopher Standish)

> January 23, 1959: Winston, Malcolm and Uncle Honey in after a hockey game from 10 to 11. (Mabel Fraser's diary)

Cookshire town hockey team, circa 1920 (Fraser family archives)

Cookshire High School champion track team, 1961 (Photo by author)

Ken loved playing baseball. We had a cousin, Jimmy McGuire, who got a contract with the Red Sox, but his career was cut short because of illness. (Bobbie Bowen)

I remember when Dad had to stop playing ball with the town. It hurt his feelings so badly because he actually got so that he couldn't run too well. He was awfully good at hitting the ball where nobody was in the field. He was able to place the ball where he wanted it to go. (Charles W.K. Fraser)

May 10, 1959: . . . Softball season opened today with band and parade from the park down to the ballpark. Doubleheader game, Daddy and I saw part of the last one. Hotel beat Turcotte's Garage, 9-1. (Mabel Fraser's diary)

July 1, 1959: . . .Went to a ball game in Bury with Dad, Malcolm and Winston. Canadiens won over Cookshire 6-0. Got some autographs. (Mabel Fraser's diary)

Montreal Canadiens players sign autographs at Dominion Day celebrations in Bury, Que., 1959 (Photo by author)

Gardening

Susie was a very early riser. Even before the sun's first morning rays announced a new day, Susie could be seen hiking up Main Street, tools in hand, to tend to her garden at Johnny Mac's home on the Wesleyville Road. After putting in a few hours planting, weeding, watering, fertilizing or harvesting – according to the season – she would return to her "day job" at Suz-Ann Beauty Parlour. Susie's enthusiasm, energy and expertise as a green-thumb gardener are recognized in the comments that follow:

Johnny Mac had a piece of land but didn't farm it. So Susie said to him "Well then, we'll farm it and make a vegetable garden." He replied, "Go ahead, go ahead." So that's exactly what she did. (Bobbie Bowen)

When I'd ask where Aunt Susie was, Uncle would say, "She left at daylight for her garden." I never knew where it was. I believe it was up the hill somewhere. (June Fraser Patterson)

From evening till morning

Susie working in her garden at sunrise (Sketch by James Harvey)

I remember stopping by the Dew Drop Inn on the way to school in the late spring and finding out that Aunt Susie had already hiked to her garden up the hill at Johnny Mac's, put in a few hours of gardening, and was back home looking after her hairdressing customers.   (John "Jack" Fraser)

Susie's garden was a wonder to behold. When I was teenager, I asked her for a little plot and she gladly gave it to me, and helped me prepare the soil, plant the seeds and care for the plants. She was also generous in sharing slips from her plants. (Betty MacRae Wright)

Susie's plants in wooden boxes hanging from the porch ceiling were a beautiful sight to behold. Her indoor plants were also a prize to see. (Dorothy Ross)

I remember my grandmother's flower and vegetable gardens. She was an excellent gardener – always had flowers in bloom. (Kerri Fraser)

Pine Hill Farm supplied manure for Susie's garden – as confirmed by Alice Fraser's always-reliable diary:

October 17, 1962: Malcolm took manure to Aunt Susie.

Malcolm loading manure for Susie's garden (Photo by author)

Fishing

Fishing was a pastime that Ken thoroughly enjoyed. Although I don't remember it, my mom's diary says he took me fishing with him on at least one occasion. Her entry for July 10, 1956 reads: "Winston went fishing with Uncle Ken. (No luck)." Maybe that's why I don't remember! But what he probably enjoyed even more than fishing was telling stories about some of his fishing partners – especially a guy from New York City whom they called "The Sergeant."

From evening till morning

My dad fished all the time. They say he was out fishing when I was born! We went fishing out towards Bury, down in the hollow, not far past the cemetery, where there was a little brook about two or three feet wide. The furthest place we fished was Ditton Brook. Dad just loved walking when we were fishing because it gave him exercise. I remember as a little kid, I'd come back from fishing in the evening and my knees and legs would ache because we'd walked so far.

And oh, there was a character from the States that we used to take fishing – some relative of my mother. His name was James Bardon but we always called him The Sergeant. He had fought in the war. He was a proud old gentleman who stood just as straight as could be, but he liked his alcohol. After he lost his New York driver's license in an alcohol-related accident, he used Uncle Fred McCormick's address in Montpelier, Vermont as a residence in order to obtain a license in Vermont. (Charles W.K. Fraser)

I want to tell you the story about a guy they called The Sergeant who used to visit from the States. He was a big guy, he wore a diamond pinky ring, and he lived in New York City in the Harlem area when Harlem was not like it is today. He would come barging through the Dew Drop Inn front door like the wind had blown it open. He would come blustering in and say, "Kenneth, Kenneth, let's go fishing." Ken replies, "I'm in the middle of doing something, I can't go fishing." Sergeant says, "No, we've got to go fishing. I'm going myself then. I want to catch some trout." He opens up his tackle box full of fishing flies. He says, "I'm going to go up there and test them out, I'll be back." So Sergeant leaves to go fishing. About an hour later, Ken heads out on the same road. Now it should be mentioned that the Sergeant was a horrible driver. He is already coming back from fishing, driving on the wrong side of the road. So Ken passes him on the wrong side to avoid colliding with him. Well, the Sergeant swerved at the last second and ends up in the ditch! Ken goes fishing, and when he comes back home at 9 o'clock that evening, Sergeant shows up at the Dew Drop. Ken asks him, "What happened?" Sergeant replies, "You want to know what happened to me today? I had some Frenchman cut me off on the road and shoved me into the ditch and just left me there!" Ken says, "Oh no, are you okay?" Sergeant responds, "Yes, but I'm just getting back now, it's 9 o'clock at night!" Ken innocently asks "Well, how do you know that the guy was a Frenchman?" Sergeant replies: "Because he was coming right at me driving on the wrong side of the road." So Ken says "In France, they drive on the same side of the road as we do. So the guy must have been an Englishman because in England they drive on the other side of the road." (Bobbie Bowen)

Here is another story about The Sergeant. Once when he was returning from a successful fishing outing, with his basket of catch in the back seat, a trout fell out of the basket and dropped down under the rear seat of his beautiful and meticulously cared-for 1936 Ford. Unbeknownst to him, the fish languished there for some time. It was in the summertime, of course, so the fish's condition deteriorated quite quickly. Poor Sergeant couldn't figure out where the stench was coming from until he discovered the rotting culprit under the rear seat! (Charles W.K. Fraser)

The Sergeant goes fishing and ends up in the ditch (Sketch by James Harvey)

Ken often told stories about finding worms in fish. (Christopher Standish)

I guess I was about 10 years old. I always remember Ken wanted to go trout fishing, and of course, I had never been trout fishing. I don't know if I was even 10 . . . Anyway, we went up to Christmas Brook, up that way somewhere. When we got there, he put me up on this gigantic rock and said "Okay, you just fish here for a while and see how you do." Well, I was up there for no more than three minutes when I caught this fish. I was so excited that I started screaming because I didn't know how to get down off the rock. Ken said to me, "We might as well go home now, because you've scared away all the fish with your yelling!" (Bobbie Bowen)

One time, up at Spider Lake, John Burton had caught a large trout – probably about a foot long. He was so happy and proud of himself as he held it up by the gills and yelled at Dad and me to take a look at his beautiful catch. Suddenly he stepped into a deep trench and threw the fish back in the water. It was a very funny sight. (Charles W.K. Fraser)

From evening till morning

> May 30, 1959: Dad went fishing. Ma and I waited on store. (Mabel Fraser's diary)

One thing Ken and Susie did **not** do in their leisure time was to attend the popular Saturday night barn dances held at venues such as Batley's, Burrough's Falls and elsewhere. According to son Charles, "Mom would have loved to go dancing – apparently she could really do the Charleston proud. But my dad was totally set against dancing of any type because he associated dancing with drinking."

Chapter 9   The fruit of her hands

Afghan handcrafted by Susie (Photo by Kerri Fraser)

The passion

Susie was not your normal sort of craftsperson who took up a hobby just for the heck of it. Nor was she a member of the local "stitch and bitch" women's group that met to gossip about their neighbours or to escape from their husbands! No, this remarkably talented woman was at least a country mile removed from such frivolous folly. Susie's needlework activities were pursued with passion and purpose. So, not surprisingly, the results of her lengthy labours of love were nothing short of perfection.

A cheery, jolly person by nature, Susie always seemed especially happy when she was working on one of her creations. Her patience and perseverance were quite remarkable, given the length of time required to complete some of her masterpieces. In an August 2000 interview with The Record, Susie states "It takes me about a month to complete a quilt in a hurry, a bit longer if I take my time."

Susie prepares for the Cookshire Fair, August 2000 (Sherbrooke Record)

One of the secrets of Susie's success was that she stitched with purpose. Every item that passed through her nimble digits had a specific destination associated with it. Perhaps it was a quilt for a relative's wedding, a woolly sweater set for a newborn, a Christmas towel for the Church bazaar or a pair of mittens for one of her grandkids. But more likely, it was something for the next edition of the annual Cookshire Fair!

Every year Susie would compete with other crafty ladies of Compton County for the title of "Handicraft Queen." And more often than not, she would earn that honour.

One might logically wonder where Susie found the time to craft all her marvellous creations. After all, she was busy with her hairdressing business all day and often well into the evening. The answer may lie in one of daughter Mabel's diary entries: "March 27, 1959: Ma very busy. Up at 2:30 a.m." There was no idle time in Susie's day because she didn't like not being busy. "I wouldn't know what to do with myself without some sewing in my hands," she told Claudia Villemaire in a 2000 interview with The Record.

The pieces

What kind of items did Susie make? The answer to this question is found in the pages of the annual Cookshire Fair book. If the article was listed under "Class 48 – Ladies Department" (or in later years under the less sexist "Class 64 – Adult Handicrafts"), chances are good that Susie probably made it at one time or another during her 60+ years of exhibiting. In her final years at the Fair, she exhibited somewhat fewer items, as she confessed to The Record's Claudia Villemaire in 2000 when she was 93 years old: "I don't have nearly as many things to take to the Fair as I used to. This year, I only have a couple pairs of socks, dresser scarves, tablecloths and a few other things, besides a couple of quilts."

On subsequent pages the complete list of 113 item categories from the 1942 Cookshire Fair book is reproduced. First prize in each category was worth a

The fruit of her hands

whopping 75 cents! By 2002, Susie's final year at the Fair, the number of item categories had been whittled down to 64 and the payout for first prize had jumped to $3.50.

Admirers, purchasers and recipients of Susie's beautiful pieces share their comments and stories following:

> I remember her absolutely beautiful quilts. (Muriel French Fitzsimmons)

> I have a rug that she made for us. We use it as a decorative wall hanging instead of a rug to step on. It has a white background with red and blue flowers – it's gorgeous. It's like crochet but not crochet – she did it with yarns. (Bobbie Bowen)

> She was knitting afghans, socks and many other items. Oh my God, that woman never stopped! I have an afghan that she knit for me when I got married. (Louise Knox)

> I won one of her afghans at a church bazaar. It was beautiful. To this day I wish I had bought one of her quilts." (Diane Fraser Keet)

> There was a neat thing that Mom learned to do when she moved to the Grace Christian Home. She didn't have a lot of space to do her needlecrafts. So she devised a system where she would use three needles instead of one. She'd go along for a few inches on one needle, then go to the next needle for the next few inches, and so on. That way, she could more easily manage larger items within the limited space of her room. (Charles W.K. Fraser)

> We have one of the last quilts that she ever made and it is on our bed today. (Greg Fraser)

One of Susie's last quilts (Photo by Greg Fraser)

CLASS 48
LADIES' DEPARTMENT

No article that has taken a first prize may be exhibited again for a prize.

All exhibits must be the work of the exhibitor, otherwise prizes will be forfeited.

Every article must be delivered to the ladies in charge not later than 11 a.m., Monday, August 24.

Judging will commence at 2 p.m., Monday, August 24.

Address all entries and communications to the Secretary of Cookshire Fair, Cookshire, Que.

Prizes in each section in this class are as follows:
1st, .75; 2nd, .50; 3rd, .35; 4th, 20

WHITE EMBROIDERY
Sec.
1. Luncheon Set or Five o'clock Tea.
2. Centrepiece.
3. Pair of Towels.
4. Pair of Pillow Slips.
5. Tray Cloth.
6. Bureau or Buffet Scraf.
7. Serviettes 4" or more under 16".
8. Taple napkins, 4 hand-hemmed and initialed.
9. Any other article.

CLASSE 48
DEPARTEMENT DES DAMES

Aucun article qui a déjà reçu un premier prix ne doit concourir.

Tout exhibit devra être fait par l'exposant, autrement les prix seront confisqués.

Chacun des articles doit être remis aux dames en charge pas plus tard que 11 heures a.m., lundi, le 24 août.

L'appréciation commencera à 2 heures p.m., lundi le 24 août.

Adressez toute entrée et correspondance au secrétaire de l'Exposition de Cookshire, Cookshire, Qué.

Les prix dans chaque section dans cette classe, sont comme suit:
1er, .75; 2ème, .50; 3ème, .35; 4ème, .20.

BRODERIE BLANCHE
Sec.
1. Set à goûter ou Nappe à thé.
2. Centre.
3. Paire de serviettes à toilette.
4. Paire d'oreillers.
5. Nappe à plateau.
6. Echarpe de bureau ou de buffet.
7. Serviettes, 4 ou plus moins de 16".
8. Serviettes à table, 4 ourlées à la main et initialées.
9. Tout autre article.

Ladies' Department prize list, Cookshire Fair 1942 – page 1 of 5

Compton County Agricultural Society No. 1

CUT WORK, WHITE

10. Teacloth or luncheon set.
11. Bureau or buffet scarf or set.
12. Pair Pillow Slips.
13. Any other article.

CUT WORK, COLORED THREAD

10a. Teacloth or luncheon set.
11a. Bureau or buffet scarf or set.
12a. Pair Pillow Slips.
13a. Any other article.

COLORED EMBROIDERY

14. Luncheon Set.
15. Centrepiece.
16. Table runner.
17. Table cover.
18. Bureau or buffet set.
19. Towel.
20. Card table cover.
21. Den set, two or more pieces.
22. Sofa cushion.
23. Any article.

CROCHET WORK IN WHITE

24. Five o'clock teacloth or luncheon set.
25. Doilies, 3 under 12", different designs.
26. Serviettes, 4 or more, under 16".
27. Centrepiece, over 12".
28. Bureau or buffet scarf or set.
29. Hot dish mats, set of 4 or more.
30. Pillow slips, with lace or insertion, or both.
31. Towels, with lace, insertion or both.
32. Collection crochet work, white, 3 pieces or more.

BRODERIE RICHELIEU, BLANCHE

10. Set à goûter ou nappe à thé.
11. Echarpe de bureau ou de buffet ou set.
12. Paire d'oreillers.
13. Tout autre article.

BRODERIE RICHELIEU, FILS COULEURS

10a. Set à goûter ou nappe à thé.
11a. Echarpe de bureau ou de buffet ou set.
12a. Paire d'oreillers.
13a. Tout autre article.

BRODERIE EN COULEUR

14. Set à goûter.
15. Centre.
16. Chemin de table.
17. Couverture de table.
18. Echarpe de bureau ou de buffet.
19. Serviette.
20. Couverture de table de jeu.
21. Set de fumoir, 2 morceaux ou plus.
22. Coussin de sofa.
23. Aucun article.

OUVRAGE AU CROCHET EN BLANC

24. Nappe à thé ou set à goûter.
25. Centres, 3 moins de 12", différents dessins.
26. Serviette, 4 ou plus, moins de 16".
27. Centre de plus de 12".
28. Echarpe de bureau ou de buffet ou set.
29. Dessus de plats chauds, 4 ou plus.
30. Taies d'oreiller, avec dentelle ou insertion, ou les deux.
31. Serviette de toilette, avec dentelle, insertion ou les deux.
32. Collection de crochet en blanc, 3 morceaux ou plus.

Ladies' Department prize list, Cookshire Fair 1942 – page 2 of 5

La Société d'Agriculture No. 1 du Comté de Compton

CROCHET WORK IN COLOUR

33. Table cover.
34. Centrepiece.
35. Table runner.
36. Sofa Cushion.
37. Door Panel.

FANCY WORK, OTHER THAN ABOVE

38. Fancy bag, any kind.
39. Large work bag.
40. Work Apron.
41. Sampler.
42. Fancy apron.
43. Italian hemstitching.
44. Silhouette, any article.
45. Hemstitching.
46. Chesterfield set.
47. Needle point.
48. Applique, any article.
49. Wool embroidery, any article.
50. Hardanger, any article.
51. Tatting, any article.
51a. Netting or hair pin lace.
52. Smocking, any article.
53. Drawn work, any article.
54. Cross stitch.
    (a) In wool on canvas.
    (b) Luncheon or tea set.
    (c) Any other article.
55. Cushion, wool knitted.
56. Cushion, wool crocheted.
57. Cushion, wool quilted.
58. Afghan, knitted.
59. Afghan, crocheted.

DOMESTIC WORK

60. 2 sk. domestic linen thread.
61. Skein wool, reversible quilt.
62. Pair men's mittens in pattern, home-spun wool.
63. Lady's Scarf, knitted or crocheted, in home-spun wool.

OUVRAGE AU CROCHET EN COULEURS

33. Couverture de table.
34. Centre.
35. Chemin de table.
36. Coussin de sofa.
37. Panneau de porte.

OUVRAGE DE FANTAISIE, AUTRE QUE CI-HAUT

38. Sac de fantaisie.
39. Grand sac à ouvrage.
40. Tablier de travail.
41. Panneau de fantaisie.
42. Tablier de fantaisie.
43. Point à jour, italien.
44. Silhouette, tout article.
45. Point à jour, article fini.
46. Set à chesterfield.
47. Point d'aiguille, article fini.
48. Appliqué, tout article.
49. Broderie en laine, tout article.
50. Hardinger, tout article.
51. Frivolité, tout article.
51a. Filet ou dentelle sur une broche à cheveu.
52. Ouvrage, découpé, tout article.
53. Ouvrage au fil tiré.
54. Point croisé.
    (a) Laine sur canevas.
    (b) Set à goûter ou set à thé.
    (c) Tout autre article.
55. Coussin, en laine tricoté.
56. Coussin, en laine crocheté.
57. Coussin, en laine piqué.
58. Alghan, tricoté.
59. Afghan, crocheté.

OUVRAGE DOMESTIQUE

60. 2 écheveaux de fil de lin domestique, chaîne et tissure.
61. Echeveau de laine, couverture reversible.
62. Une paire de mitaines, à patron, pour homme, laine domestique.
63. Une écharpe pour dame, tricot à la broche ou au crochet, laine domestique.

Ladies' Department prize list, Cookshire Fair 1942 – page 3 of 5

64. Lady's shawl or sweater, fancy knitting, in home-spun wool.
65. Men's sweater.
66. Hooked rug, scenery or pattern.
67. Woven stair carpet, at least 6 yards.
68. Doormat, half moon in floral design.
69. Homespun cloth, pure wool, for young girl's autumn coat.
70. Chest cover, in cross weaving, about 45" x 60", pure homespun wool.
71. Pair of kitchen curtains, in pure domestic linen, natural or coloured, any pattern.
72. Piece of linen for toweling, pure homespun linen, at least 3 yards.
73. Baby's dress, with fancy work, (smocking, fagotting or embroidery).
74. Table cover, made from cotton bags, average size.
75. Centrepiece, crocheted, cotton or mercerized thread, 8 to 10 inches.
76. Piece of rag carpeting, fancy pattern.
77. Coverlet, knit from ravelled wool.
78. Woven tablecloth with 4 serviettes.
79. Bedroom set, any material.
80. Silk quilt.
81. Patchwork quilt, worsted.
82. Patchwork quilt, cotton or print.
83. Bed coverlet, crocheted.
84. Bed coverlet, knitted.
85. Bed coverlet, embroidered.
86. Bed coverlet, home woven.

64. Un chandail onglet pour dames, laine domestique, filage de fantaisie.
65. Chandail d'homme.
66. Un tapis crocheté, genre pièce mûrale, paysage, catalogne.
67. Un tapis d'escalier, catalogne, au moins 6 verges de longueur.
68. Un tapis de porte, demi-lune, dessin floral, catalogne.
69. Une pièce de tissu à manteau d'automne, pour jeune fille, pure laine domestique.
70. Une couverture de voiture, tissage croisé, 45" x 60" environ, pure laine domestique.
71. Une paire de rideaux de cuisine, pur lin domestique, naturel ou teint, modèle au choix.
72. Une pièce de toile croisée, pour serviettes, pur lin domestique, au moins 3 verges.
73. Une robe de bébé, travail de fantaisie à la main (nid d'abeilles, points de fagot, broderie, etc).
74. Une nappe faite de sacs de coton, grandeur moyenne.
75. Un centre, tricoté au crochet, coton ou fil mercerisé, 8 à 10 pouces de diamètre.
76. Une catalogne, à patron.
77. Couverte tricotée avec de la laine usagée.
78. Nappe tissée, avec 4 serviettes.
79. Parure de chambre à coucher, matériel au choix.
80. Couvre-pied en soie.
81. Couvre-pieds en laine rapiéceté.
82. Couvre-pieds en coton rapiéceté.
83. Couvre-pieds crocheté.
84. Couvre-pieds tricoté.
85. Couvre-pieds brodé.
86. Couvre-pieds tissé au métier.

Ladies' Department prize list, Cookshire Fair 1942 – page 4 of 5

La Société d'Agriculture No. 1 du Comté de Compton

87. Pair blankets, home woven.
88. Rug, braided.
89. Yarn, single woollen.
90. Yarn, double and twisted.
91. Pair wool gloves, for men.
92. Pair wool gloves, for women.
93. Pair child's mittens, or gloves.
94. Sweater, child's.
95. Pair Ladies' wool stockings.
96. Pair men's wool socks, lightweight.
97. Pair men's wool socks, heavy.
98. Pair child's stockings.
99. Pair ladies' woolen mittens.
100. Pair men's woolen mittens.
101. Five yards, cloth, home spun, any kind.
102. Bed jacket.
103. Knitted sweater, adult's.
104. Knitted or crocheted shawl scarf.
105. Baby's set, knitted.
106. Baby's set, crocheted.
107. Pair woolen socks. (tennis).

WORK DONE BY LADIES 75 YEARS OLD

108. Knitting.
109. Embroidery.
110. Patch work.
111. Rug, any kind.
112. Tatting.
113. Crocheting.

87. Couvertures, paire, faites au métier.
88. Tapis natté.
89. Laine simple.
90. Laine double et tordue.
91. Paire de gants de laine pour hommes.
92. Paire de gants de laine pour dames.
93. Paire de mitaines pour enfants ou gants.
94. Chandail pour enfants.
95. Paire de bas de laine pour dames.
96. Paire de bas de laine, légers, pour hommes.
97. Paire de bas de laine, pesant, pour hommes.
98. Paire de bas pour enfants.
99. Paire de mitaines en laine pour dames.
100. Paire de mitaines en laine pour hommes.
101. Cinq verges de drap fait au métier, à la maison, aucune sorte.
102. Frileuse.
103. Chandail tricoté pour adultes.
104. Châle ou écharpe, tricoté ou crocheté.
105. Set de bébé, 3 morceaux, tricoté.
106. Set de bébé, crocheté.
107. Paire de bas de laine (tennis.)

OUVRAGE FAIT PAR DAMES DE 75 ANS OU PLUS

108. Tricotage.
109. Broderie.
110. Rapiècetage.
111. Tapis, aucune sorte.
112. Ouvrage de frivolité.
113. Ouvrage au crochet.

Ladies' Department prize list, Cookshire Fair 1942 – page 5 of 5

The fruit of her hands

Examples of Susie's handiwork. Clockwise from top left:
needlepoint (Marilyn Fraser Reed); afghan (Karen Fraser Jackson);
quilt (Marilyn Fraser Reed); embroidery (Marilyn Fraser Reed)

She also made items as ordinary as socks and gloves. She even had a stocking machine for making stockings more easily but she never had much of a chance to use it. She always did them by hand. (Charles W.K. Fraser)

The prizes

Susie Fraser exhibited her creations at the Cookshire Fair for 67 consecutive years beginning in 1936. And every year she came away with a bagful of prize ribbons (actually they were prize cards), most of which were red in colour. After the Fair was over, Susie would sell many of her items, often with the prize tags attached. She was justifiably proud of her achievements. Family and friends share their memories of Susie's prize-winning entries:

> I have many of her quilts and fancywork items – all first prize winners at the Fair. (Kerri Fraser)

> Aunt Susie possessed remarkable needlework skills. Phil bought one of her gorgeous bedspreads for me. Every single stitch was painstakingly laid down by hand. Not surprisingly, it won first prize at the Cookshire Fair. I have the actual red first prize card. I possess another red tag item – a patchwork banner celebrating Canada's 125th anniversary. Also, I have a beautifully crafted cross stitch image of birds adorning a tree branch. This was given to me by Charles after his parents had both died. He distributed a few treasures and mementoes to some of us the last time that he and Myrna attended our annual Fraser Reunion. (Marilyn Fraser Reed)

> I remember buying at least five of her quilts, one each for my three nephews and two for employees as wedding gifts. The employees had been students of Mabel in Ayer's Cliff. The quilts all had been first place winners at the Cookshire Fair. I also bought as gifts some baby blankets that she made while living at Grace Christian Home in Huntingville. (Rodger Heatherington)

> When I went to Cookshire Fair I always checked out Susie's crafts. She won so many ribbons. (Dorothy Shelton Dionne)

> I never purchased any of Susie's work but I did view a lot of it at the fairgrounds. Very nice work. I think she also donated some of her work to the annual Anglican Church "white elephant sale." (Almon Pope)

> I remember talking to Susie upstairs at the Fair and admiring her beautiful handiwork. (Theda Jackson Lowry)

> Cookshire Fair is one of the oldest of its kind. It bears witness firstly to English Canadian community life. Mrs. Fraser's involvement in the Fair illustrates her total integration in the community, its vision and its objectives. (Jean-François Nadeau)

The fruit of her hands

Susie Fraser First Prize card on quilt; Susie's Canada 125 banner (Courtesy of Marilyn Fraser Reed)

Susie's handicrafts exhibited at Cookshire Fair (Photo by author)

In addition to competing at the Fair, Susie also sponsored special prizes for several years during the 1950s and 1960s. A few examples of her support:

- 1951: Best quilt, silk, wool, or cotton: Mdse $1.25 $0.75

- 1958: Highest aggregate in class 48, sections 31-59: Mdse $1.25 $0.75 (This included crochet work and some other fancy work.)

- 1960-1965: Highest aggregate in class 48, sections 31-46a: Mdse $1.25 $0.75 (This included crochet work.)

Susie's handicrafts at the Cookshire Fair, 1989 (Photo by author)

Susie cuts cake for her 95th Birthday, 2002
(Photo by Jim Fraser)

Chapter 10   The rumble of wheels

Railroad fan

Ken Fraser was the quintessential railroad fan. Some might even say that he was a railroad fanatic. He loved everything to do with trains. Maybe it was the rumble of the wheels of the mighty steam locomotives. Perhaps it was the sheer excitement of train travel. Or yet still, it might have been the mystery of Morse code telegraph communications. But more likely, it was in his blood and in his DNA.

George Gill and steam train at Cookshire station, 1957 (Photo by Jim Shaughnessy, The Call of Trains)

Ken was exposed to trains and the railroad long before the days of Dew Drop Inn. His Pine Hill Farm birthplace, which bordered the Canadian Pacific Railway main line between Montreal and Halifax, afforded an excellent view of the passing trains. In fact the windows of his family's brick house would literally shake and

View of Pine Hill Farm from the C.P.R. tracks, circa 1958 (Photo by author)

C.P.R. steam locomotives, Cookshire, circa 1954 (Photo by author)

rattle as the steam locomotives powered their way up the steep grade toward Birchton. Perhaps young Ken dreamed of riding on those trains one day, or of working on the railroad when he grew up. Son Charles, however, attributes his dad's great interest in all things "railroad" to something else that happened years later.

> Dad's interest in trains and the railroad goes back to when he worked in Sherbrooke for the CPR redoing the roundhouse – or building it from scratch. He worked for a Mr. Dingman setting ties and setting rails. In those days it was all bull work – there were no lifts. Dad said that it was

very heavy work. This job lasted only a short while before he was laid off. (Charles W.K. Fraser)

Railroad roundhouse, Midland, Colorado (www. pinterest.ca)

Whatever its origins, Ken's fascination with the railroad was genuine and lifelong. He subscribed to various railroad-related magazines including Trains, Railroad and others. As illustrated below, he maintained correspondence with at least one of them, seeking information or correcting erroneous information that had been printed in a previous issue.

> Long-time reader Ken Fraser of Cookshire, Que., Canada, says Michael Eagleson's January cover photo was taken in Victoriaville, Que., not Victorville. Ken has ridden on two fan-trips pulled by the engine shown in that photo, has many pix of her. (Railroad Magazine, Volumes 85-86, 1969, page 35)

> Information on the Colorado, Silver Springs & Cripple Creek District of more than 50 years ago is wanted by Ken Fraser, Cookshire, Que., Canada. (Railroad Magazine, Volumes 85-86, 1969, page 41)

When the railroads converted from steam to diesel in the 1950s some of the traditional railroad sounds were silenced forever. Ken's daughter, Mabel, recognizing her dad's nostalgia for these sounds, gave him a special gift that she mentions in her diary entry of April 26, 1959: "I bought Dad a record of train sounds."

Friends and neighbours have also recognized Ken's love affair with trains and the railroad:

> Ken often talked about trains and the railway station. I think he would have liked working on the railroad. (Dorothy Shelton Dionne)

> I remember Ken's love of trains. (Ben Hodge)

> Ken was crazy about trains. (Rev. Ron West)

Model trains

Unfortunately I never got to see my uncle's pride and joy elaborate electric train setup that was hidden away in his third storey attic. However, I have heard many glowing reports about it, especially since beginning my research for this book. Even though I never climbed the ladder to behold the magic above, I remember seeing various individual pieces of rolling stock displayed in Dew Drop Inn's large glass showcase. There were locomotives, cabooses and boxcars among others. I believe that most of his collection were Lionel HO gauge 1:87 scale units.

Model train (www.lionel.com)

It seems that access to the attic display was limited to a privileged few. One such visit was noted in Mabel's diary of September 10, 1959: "Dad and boys up to see trains in the attic." Following are the recollections of people who actually did view Ken's awesome attic arrangement:

> I had a very special privilege with Ken. He took me up into the attic and showed me his model railroad setup. We went up a ladder to get in there. I asked him why he kept it so well hidden and his response was, "You know, Reverend, if a lot of other people saw me, they'd think I was a bit crazy playing with trains like this." But I said, "No way." He had a spectacular setup – with bridges and tunnels. The trains were really beautiful. They went around the track and there were train whistles and crossing bells. (Rev. Ron West)

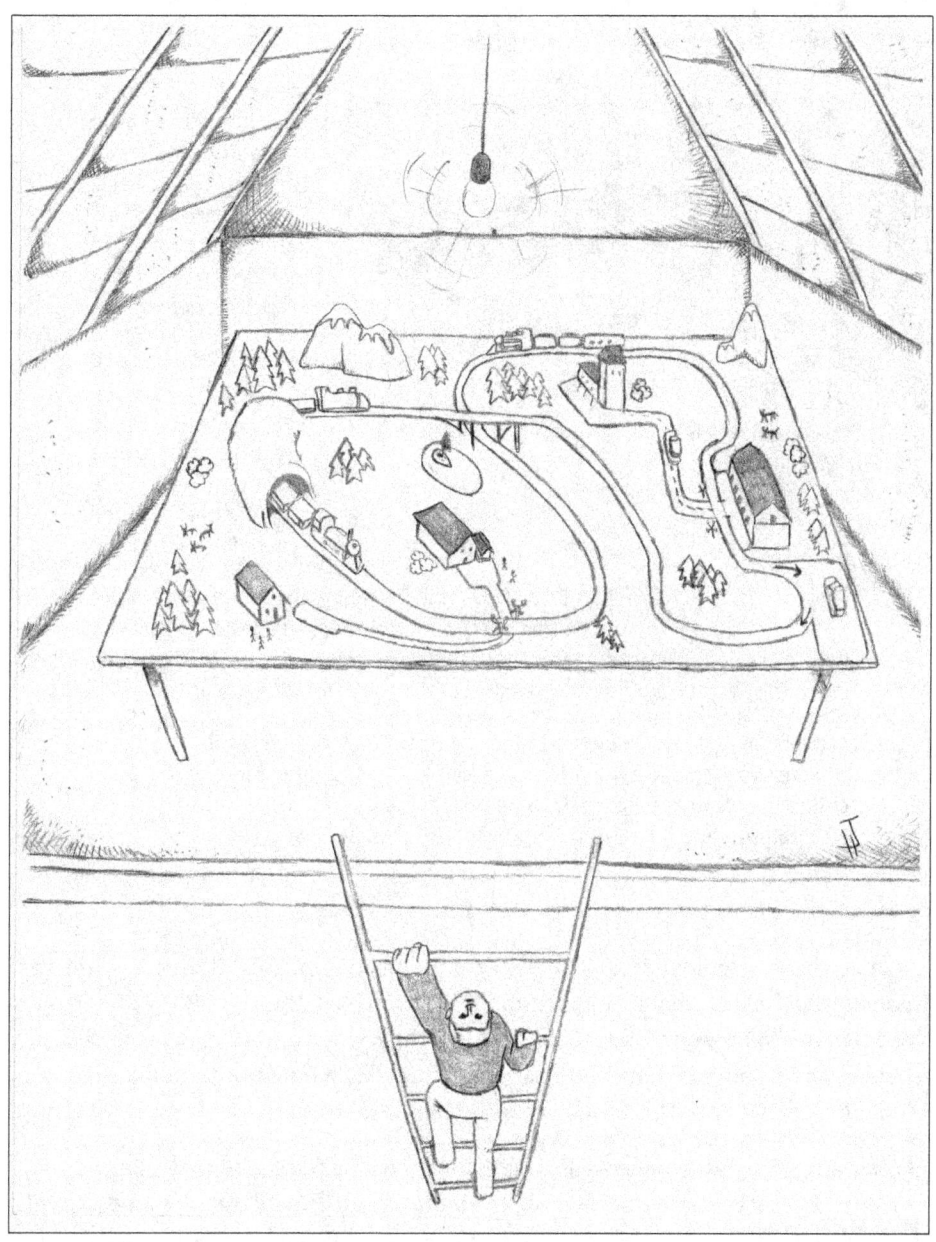
Ken's model train setup in Dew Drop Inn's attic (Sketch by James Harvey)

Dew Drop Inn

Ken attending a model train show, circa 1960 (Fraser family archives)

Both my sisters and I remember Ken's amazing model train set up in the attic. As a favour to my father, John French, he showed us the trains and had them run on the tracks. The whole train setup was magical to us little girls. (Muriel French Fitzsimmons)

Once I even climbed that ladder into the attic where Uncle had his model trains set up. They were magnificent. (June Fraser Patterson)

One of my memories of Dew Drop Inn is being up in the attic with Charles and Ken, in awe of Ken's large model railroad layout. Often Ken would be at the kitchen table assembling a freight car or other rolling stock for the layout. (Stan Parker)

I remember having Uncle Ken take me upstairs and then climbing up into the attic where I saw and marvelled at his magnificent electric train collection, with the lights flashing and those special locomotives that he had painted and labelled so expertly. (John "Jack" Fraser)

Real trains

As much as Ken enjoyed playing with the miniature models, it was the life-size models that really kindled his passion. Like watching the double-header steam locomotives thunder through Cookshire on their way to Halifax or Montreal. Or reading about famous Canadian trains like the Newfie Bullet or the Confederation Train. Anything to do with trains interested and excited him.

Something that must have really made Ken's heart pound was when he received news of a spectacular derailment near Birchton. He immediately jumped into his car, collected a few people and raced to the scene of the train wreck. My mom's diary entry for November 25, 1951 records the event: "Dad & John went to see train wreck at Birchton with Kenneth." One of those who accompanied Ken to the site recalls the experience:

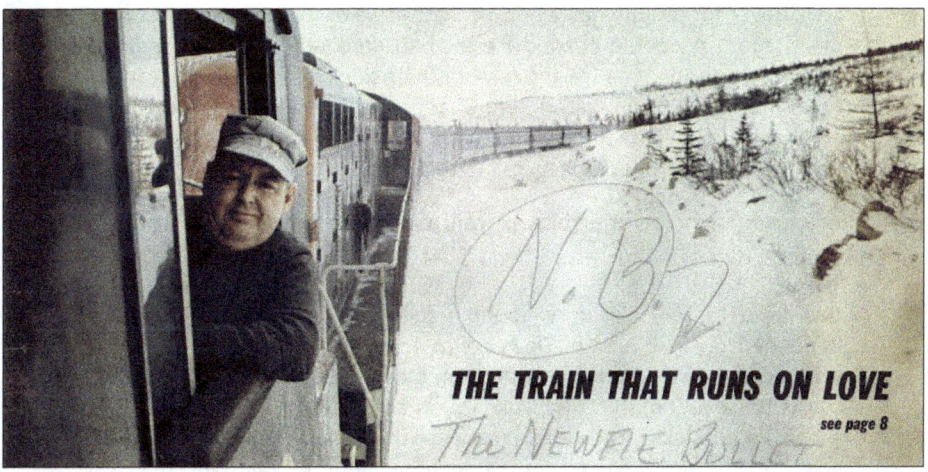

Clipping re: Newfie Bullet, Weekend Magazine, Feb . 1, 1969 (Fraser family archives)

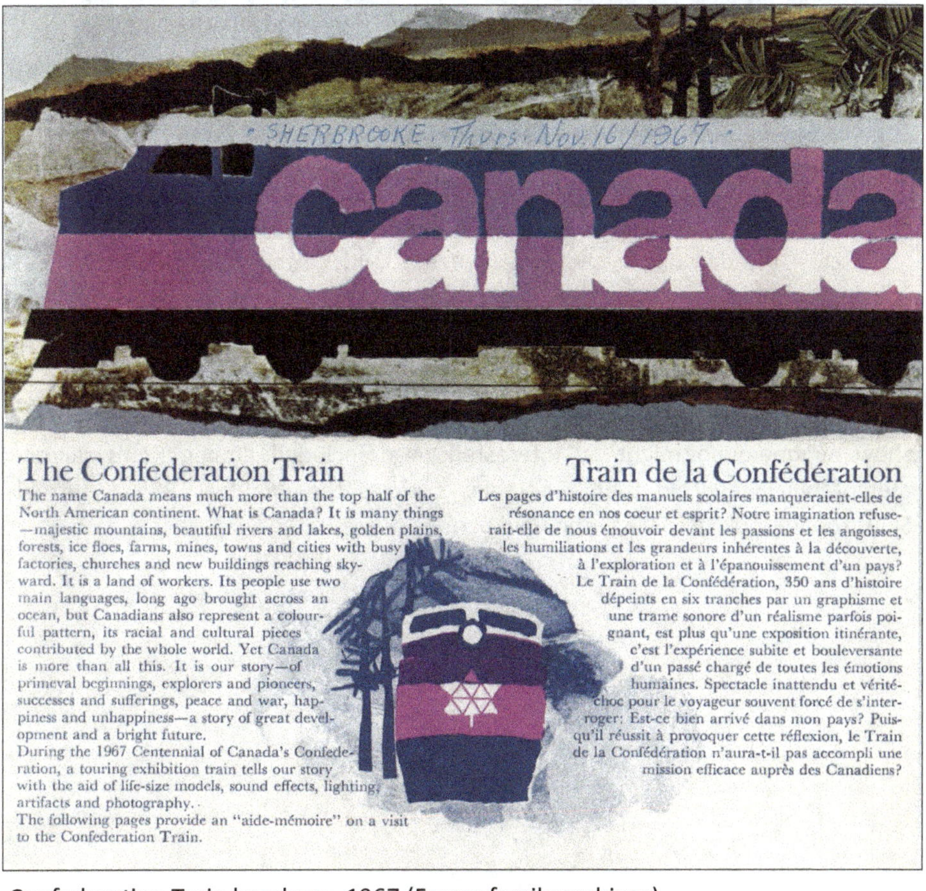

The Confederation Train

The name Canada means much more than the top half of the North American continent. What is Canada? It is many things —majestic mountains, beautiful rivers and lakes, golden plains, forests, ice floes, farms, mines, towns and cities with busy factories, churches and new buildings reaching skyward. It is a land of workers. Its people use two main languages, long ago brought across an ocean, but Canadians also represent a colourful pattern, its racial and cultural pieces contributed by the whole world. Yet Canada is more than all this. It is our story—of primeval beginnings, explorers and pioneers, successes and sufferings, peace and war, happiness and unhappiness—a story of great development and a bright future.
During the 1967 Centennial of Canada's Confederation, a touring exhibition train tells our story with the aid of life-size models, sound effects, lighting, artifacts and photography.
The following pages provide an "aide-mémoire" on a visit to the Confederation Train.

Train de la Confédération

Les pages d'histoire des manuels scolaires manqueraient-elles de résonance en nos coeur et esprit? Notre imagination refuserait-elle de nous émouvoir devant les passions et les angoisses, les humiliations et les grandeurs inhérentes à la découverte, à l'exploration et à l'épanouissement d'un pays? Le Train de la Confédération, 350 ans d'histoire dépeints en six tranches par un graphisme et une trame sonore d'un réalisme parfois poignant, est plus qu'une exposition itinérante, c'est l'expérience subite et bouleversante d'un passé chargé de toutes les émotions humaines. Spectacle inattendu et vérité-choc pour le voyageur souvent forcé de s'interroger: Est-ce bien arrivé dans mon pays? Puisqu'il réussit à provoquer cette réflexion, le Train de la Confédération n'aura-t-il pas accompli une mission efficace auprès des Canadiens?

Confederation Train brochure, 1967 (Fraser family archives)

> I will never forget one day when Ken got news of a train wreck just west of Birchton. A double-headed freight had derailed and left two steam locomotives and some freight cars on their sides in the woods. A steam boiler had run low on water. Ken, Charles and I hopped in the car to go and have a look. Somehow we got very close to the wreck and I imagine Ken got some very good pictures. (Stan Parker)

Ken possessed a whole repertoire of railroad-related stories he would tell. Son Charles recalls two of them:

> Dad used to tell this story about a fellow named Dewey Daniels. It happened up in Birchton. Dewey was trying to move a flatcar full of railroad ties. The flatcar got away from him and started rolling down the tracks toward Cookshire. Because it was so heavily loaded, it picked up speed very quickly. They said that when it went by your folks' farm, it was literally whistling. At the same time, another railroad crew was working with a pile driver on a bridge just beyond Cookshire. They could hear the flatcar coming because it was making such a loud whistling noise. Everybody was able to jump out of the way but the rocketing flatcar ran right over the pile driver on the bridge and smashed it all to smithereens. Fortunately nobody was hurt but poor Dewey was transferred to another division for his misdeed!

> With regard to the terrible Lac Mégantic rail disaster of 2013, I remember Dad telling me about a somewhat similar incident that happened back in the 1920s. A train got away in Milan, and went all the way down to Lake Megantic where it smashed into a whole bunch of rail cars. My dad had a photograph of the tender sitting on top of the locomotive.

Often Ken would cut out a railroad-related story or photo from a magazine or newspaper and hang the clipping on the wall behind the Dew Drop Inn counter. These items never gathered dust because they would frequently be taken down to show anyone who might be interested. Also included among Ken's railroad memorabilia were old train timetables such as the one for CPR's Montreal-Sherbrooke-Cookshire-Megantic-Halifax run.

Birchton train wreck, November 25, 1951 (Photos from the author's collection)

CANADIAN PACIFIC

N.B.

For British Columbia the outlook was never brighter

The crew working on this cut into the Corey Brothers' tunnel continually faced the extreme hazards of enormous falling rocks, toppled by another crew working above.

By Pierre Berton

IT IS NEW YEAR'S Day, 1871, the year in which Canada will become a trans-continental nation, and in most of British North America it is bitterly cold. In Ottawa, where it is 18 below, the snow, gritty as sand, squeaks eerily beneath the felted feet of morning churchgoers. A cutting wind, blowing off Lake Ontario, is heaping great drifts against the square logs of the Upper Canadian barns, smothering the snake fences and frustrating the Grand Trunk's Montreal-Toronto passenger schedule. On the St. Lawrence, in front of Quebec City, that annual phenomenon, the ice bridge, is taking form. In the harbor of Saint John, the rime hangs thickly upon the rigging, turning schooners and barquentines into ghost ships.

Only at the colonial extremities is New Year's Day a green one. In the English gardens of Victoria, the occasional yellow wallflower still blooms shyly, and in the verdant colony of Prince Edward Island the fields are free of frost. The editorial comments are as salubrious as the climate. The potato farmers of Souris and Summerside read their Saturday Islander with approval: "In our cozy little Island we have scarcely experienced anything but the blessings of Providence," it

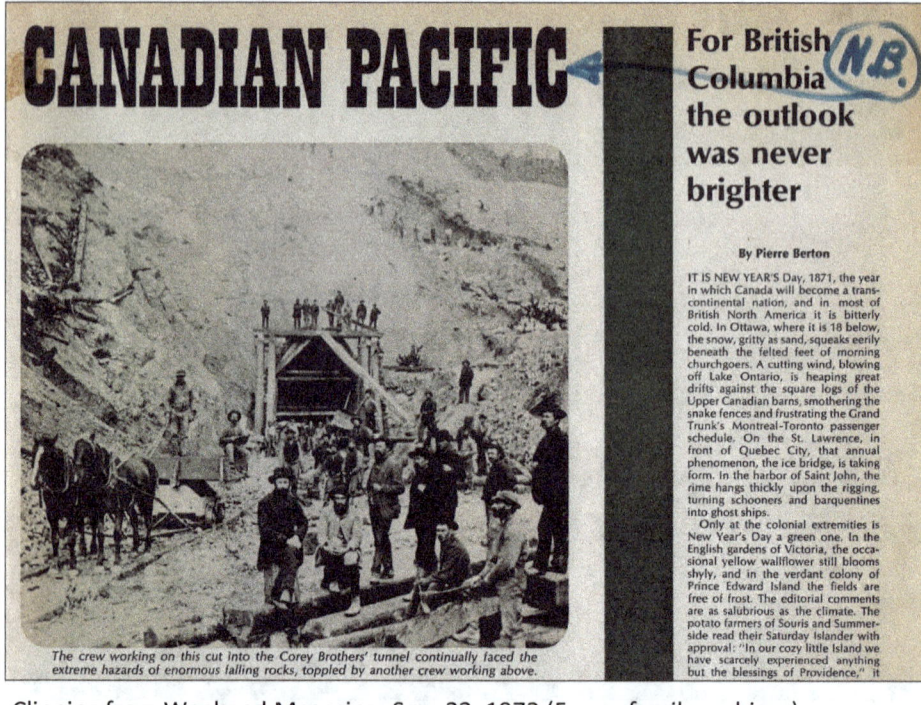

Clipping from Weekend Magazine, Sep. 23, 1972 (Fraser family archives)

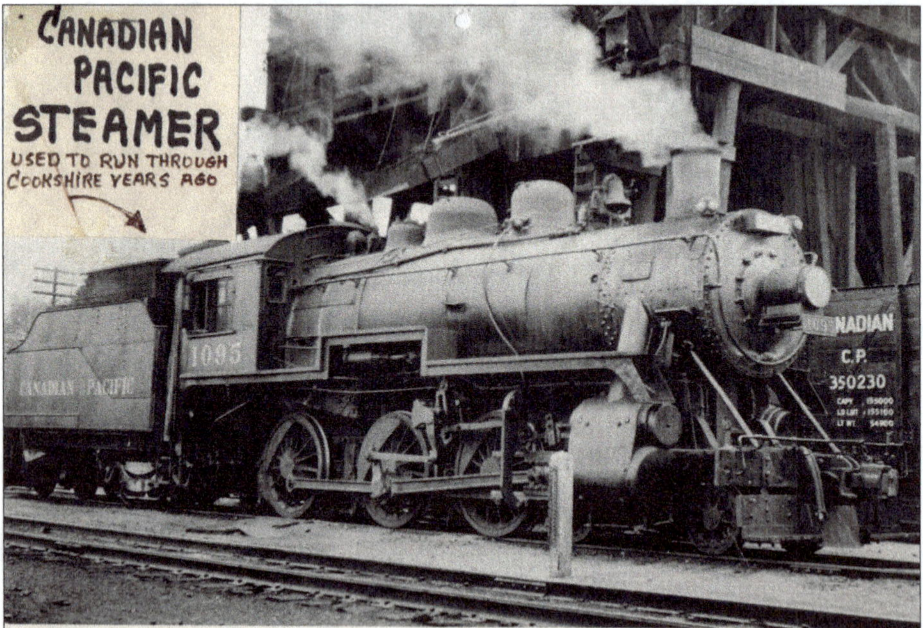

Canadian Pacific #1095,m a 4-6-0 being coaled at London, Ontario, Canada. May, 1959.

Wm. O. Gibson

Photograph of C.P.R. steam locomotive, labelled KEEP (Courtesy of Stan Parker)

The rumble of wheels

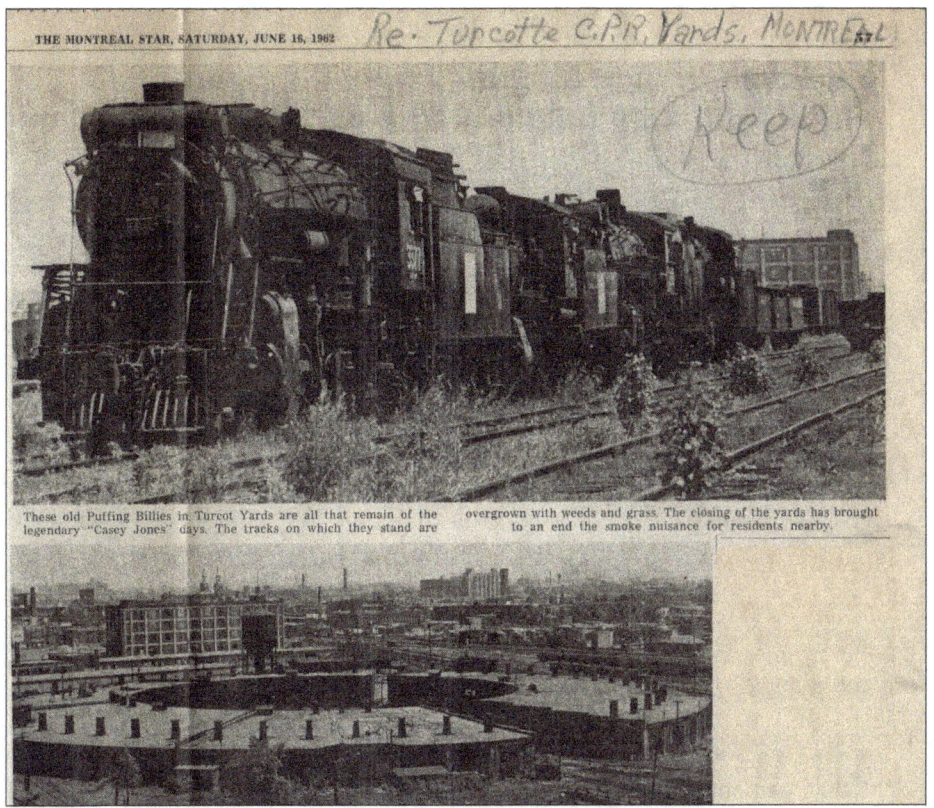

Clipping re: closing of Turcot Yards in Montreal, 1962 (Fraser family archives)

The station

Ken spent a lot of time at the Cookshire train station – collecting or delivering passengers, watching the trains, or just "hanging out." He loved chatting with the station's telegraph operators, the train conductors and line workers. Many of them he knew personally. Following are some other station-related recollections:

> Mr. Harding, a commercial traveller, would arrive on the train. Dad would meet him at the station and take him everywhere. Mr. Sweet was a conductor on the train. (Charles W.K. Fraser)

> I never met this man but Ken told me many stories about Jim Shaughnessy. An American from New York State, he's a renowned railroad photographer. At the time I think it was a hobby. Over the years he has photographed trains all over the U.S.A. and Canada, and is well published with books and magazines of railroading. He still writes a regular feature in one of the train magazines that I subscribe to. At that time in the late 1940s and early 1950s, he would drive up to Cookshire, stay at Ken's and go up and down the railroad between Sherbrooke and

Dew Drop Inn

C.P.R passenger train timetable, 1972

Top: front cover

Right: Enlargement of Montreal to St. John, N.B. timetable

(Fraser family archives)

Montréal | Farnham | Saint John

Read down/De haut en bas — Read up/De bas en haut

42 Daily Quot.	214 Note A Ex. Sat. & Sun. Sam. & dim. exc.		Station (E.T.–Eastern Time / A.T.–Atlantic Time / HE–Heure de l'Est / AT–Heure de l'Atlantique)	213 Note A Ex. Sat. & Sun. Sam. & dim. exc.	41 Daily Quot.
			Gare Windsor Stn.		
19 50	17 31	ET/HE Dp.	Montréal .. Ar	07 50	08 50
z 19 57	17 36	"	... Westmount	07 43	08 42
z 20 05	17 42	"	... Montreal West	07 37	08 35
..	17 47	"	... LaSalle	07 30	..
..	f 17 50	"	... Adirondack Jct.	f 07 28	..
..	17 56	"	... St. Constant	07 20	..
..	17 59	"	... Delson	07 17	..
..	f 18 04	"	... St. Philippe	f 07 11	..
..	f 18 11	"	... Lacadie	f 07 01	..
20 36	18 18	"	... St. Johns	06 56	07 53
..	18 21	"	... Iberville	06 51	..
..	f 18 25	"	... St. Gregoire	f 06 47	..
..	f 18 27	"	... Versailles	f 06 45	..
..	f 18 31	"	... Ste. Brigide	f 06 43	..
20 54	18 40	"	... Farnham	06 40	07 35
f 21 08		"	... Adamsville		f 07 18
f 21 17		"	... Bromont		f 07 10
f 21 29		"	... Foster		f 06 58
f 22 02		"	... Magog		f 06 30
22 30		" Ar.	Sherbrooke .. Dp (Hôtellerie Le Baron)		06 05
22 40		" Dp.	Sherbrooke .. Ar		05 55
f 23 15		"	... Cookshire		f 05 15
f 23 51		"	... Scotstown		f 04 37
00 30		" Ar.	Megantic, Que. .. Dp		04 00
00 40		" Dp.	Megantic, Que. .. Ar		03 50
01 54		"	... Jackman, Me.		02 37
f 02 48		"	... Greenville		f 01 35
03 45		" Ar.	Brownville Jct. .. Dp		00 40
03 55		" Dp.	Brownville Jct. .. Ar		00 30
04 50		"	... Mattawamkeag		23 35
f 05 31		"	... Danforth		f 22 52
06 05		" Ar.	Vanceboro, Me. .. Dp		22 15
06 10		" Dp.	Vanceboro, Me. .. Ar		22 10
07 25		AT/HA "	... McAdam, N.B. ⓜ Dp		23 00
07 40		" Dp.	McAdam, N.B. .. Ar		22 45
08 05		"	... Harvey		22 13
08 35		" Ar.	Fredericton Jct. .. Dp		21 50
tb 09 30		" Ar	Fredericton { Dp		tb 20 45
tb 07 35		" Dp	{ Ar		tb 22 40
08 35		" Dp.	Fredericton Jct. .. Ar		21 50
u 09 18		"	... Westfield Beach		...
09 45		" Ar.	Saint John .. Dp		20 50

(Will not operate Mondays Dec. 25, Jan. 1 and Fri. April 20. Ne circulera pas les lundis, 25 déc., 1 jan. et ven. 20 avril.)

In order to provide connection for passengers arriving Montreal in The Canadian and proceeding to points served by Train No. 42, the latter train will be held a maximum of 15 minutes at Montreal West.

Pour assurer la correspondance des passagers arrivant à Montréal à bord du Canadien et se dirigeant vers des points desservis par le train numéro 42, ce dernier s'arrêtera à Montréal-Ouest pendant 15 minutes au maximum.

Equipment

Trains 41 and 42—Selection of sleeping car accommodation. Coaches. (meal service).
Trains 213 and 214—Air-conditioned Rail Diesel Car.

Matériel

Trains 41 et 42—Choix de voitures-lits. Voitures-coach. (service de repas).
Trains 213 et 214—Autorail climatisé.

4

Vintage photo of Union Station, Cookshire (www.townshipsheritage.com)

Steam locomotive at Cookshire station, circa 1957 (Photo by author)

Megantic taking pictures of trains. He took a wonderful picture of George Gill loading his horse-drawn wagon with coal from a parked gondola on the siding at Cookshire, with a steam engine under a full head of steam heading across the crossing in the background. This was taken in January 1957. (Stan Parker)

Dad would hang around the station a lot. He knew the different Morse code operators. I used to go down there too and watch the guy type out the orders. One of the operators was Ivan Savaria who later opened a jewellery store in East Angus. (Charles W.K. Fraser)

Morse key telegraph device (www.sparkmuseum.com)

May 2, 1959: Dad down to station to talk to as. op. (Mabel Fraser's diary)

May 5, 1962: Ken took Verna to Dayliner at 4 PM. (Alice Fraser's diary)

December 31, 1968: Uncle Ken met me at Cookshire Station. (Alice Fraser's diary)

Dayliner at Cookshire station, circa 1962 (Photo by author)

Abandoned stationmaster's office, Cookshire station, circa 1992 (Photo by author)

In September 1994 the Cookshire railroad station, which at one time saw up to 20 trains per day, was demolished. In his October 27, 1994 Journal Le Haut-Saint-François article entitled "The Cookshire Station is no more," Claude Leclerc observed that the station's demolition also marked the end of the railroad era that had thrived in the mid-1900s. It was good that Ken Fraser, who passed away less than a year earlier, did not have to witness this sad destruction of a place that meant so much to him.

Chapter 11   A time for everything

Susie and Ken, circa 1975 (Fraser family archives)

When family and friends were asked what adjectives they would use to individually describe Ken and Susie, the answers were very interesting. Among the many characteristics and qualities suggested for each of them, there were several that were common to both:

- Susie: welcoming, friendly, generous, devoted and faithful
- Ken: welcoming, friendly, generous, caring and talkative

These shared qualities were reflected in how Ken and Susie lived their lives and how they related to the people around them. In a nutshell, they were a couple who cared deeply about people and consistently showed it.

Time for family

A few years after launching the Dew Drop Inn business, Ken and Susie were blessed with their second bundle of joy in the person of Charles Ward Kenneth. (His older sister Mabel had been born several years earlier in Sherbrooke before they moved to Cookshire.)

As busy as they both were with their multiple simultaneous occupations described in the previous chapters, Ken and Susie always had time for family. Whether for a meal, for an activity or just for a visit, they always made you feel welcome – as attested by generations of their kin. Some of their grandchildren share their early memories here:

> They were my grandparents. I always looked forward to spending my childhood summers there in the late 1960s and early 1970s. What I remember most were all the interesting places and things to explore as a child – numerous artifacts, items, rooms, etc. My grandfather would play baseball with me and my brother. My grandmother would cook all of our favorite

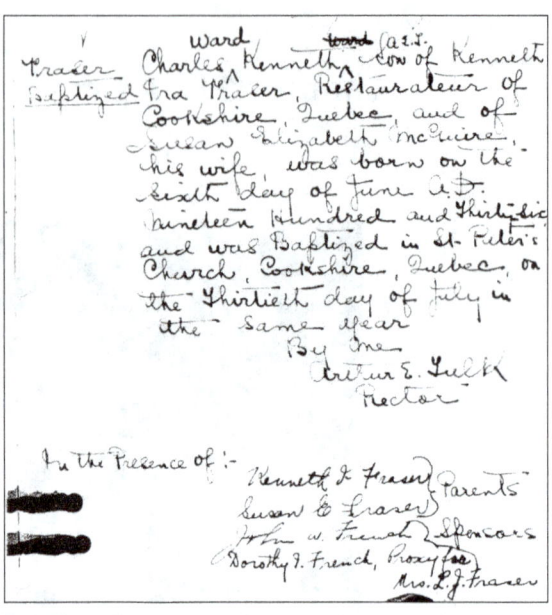

Charles Ward Kenneth Fraser baptismal certificate 1936 (Fraser family archives)

Young Charles on Dew Drop Inn steps, circa 1938 (Fraser family archives)

A time for everything

Young Charles on Dew Drop Inn steps, circa 1942 (Fraser family archives)

foods. We played cribbage with my grandfather when he visited our home. (Greg Fraser)

My earliest memories of the Dew Drop Inn are from when I was between two and three, of being put in the high chair to have dinner. We were there so often when I was younger, I used to find it strange when we didn't go down for the weekend. I love my memories of that time – mostly the 1970s I guess. Business wasn't as thriving as it had once been, but it was always a busy place, with people coming and going all the time. If my life were that busy, my head would spin! Our

Ken and Susie with great-grandchildren, circa 1992 (Fraser family archives)

memories and treasures are highly prized in our lives. I don't know of anyone else whose grandparents had a life like mine did. Some of it might be the sentimental memories of youth, but that's fine. They are warm memories. (Kerri Fraser)

Ken and Susie with Mabel and her husband Mac (Fraser family archives)

Susie (third from left) with eight of nine siblings, 1949 (Courtesy of Johnny Scholes)

A time for everything

Ken and Susie did not limit their attention to their own children and grandchildren. They offered their same warm welcome to members of their extended family who came to visit. As well, they often travelled to visit relatives far and near.

Ken and Susie with Susie's sister Nellie Scholes and Nellie's son Johnny, 1975 (Courtesy of Johnny Scholes)

Their "Fraser 12" nephews and nieces and their offspring share their memories of the Dew Drop Inn and of the enjoyable visits "out back" in the kitchen. Marina, the eldest of the Fraser 12, who passed away in 2009, had a special relationship with Ken as they shared the same birthday, December 3.

> There was strong coffee and cribbage at 2 a.m. in Uncle Ken's kitchen. (Marina Fraser Tracy, from the Christmas 1992 issue of the Fraser Family Link)

> As young kids, we never knew what was going on in the kitchen because it was sort of hidden behind the counter. (John "Jack" Fraser)

> I remember watching TV (Laurence Welk and Red Skelton) upstairs in the living room, then falling asleep and waking up to find myself alone enjoying Dew Drop Inn's delicious coffee. (Malcolm "Mac" Fraser, from the Christmas 1994 issue of the Fraser Family Link)

Every Sunday after Sunday school and/or church, we'd drop in to visit Uncle Ken. Usually five or six of us would be together for a little chat. If we were lucky, we'd have money to buy something, but usually Uncle would give us a treat if there were no other customers around. (Marilyn Fraser Reed)

I recall dropping in at Dew Drop Inn for a visit during school hours when I should have been in Mr. McGerrigle's physics class.

> I remember feeling like a big shot every time I'd go behind the counter and into the kitchen to see Aunt Susie and generally Mabel and Mac. (Warren Fraser)

After I moved away from Cookshire, when back in town I would pay a visit to the Dew Drop and get invited into the kitchen to chat with both of them. (Jim Fraser)

Ken and Marina Fraser Tracy celebrate their mutual birthday, 1992 (Fraser family archives)

I remember in school years, going into Dew Drop Inn and visiting with Uncle Ken and Aunt Susie and George Willard the bus driver. (Karen Fraser Jackson)

I remember dropping in every week after Sunday school. Two or three dogs would be jumping up and down impatiently on the tables and benches in front of the window, waiting for Aunt Susie to appear. They didn't seem to bother Johnny Mac too much as he was having his lunch. On our way home as we walked along Craig Street approaching Fraser Road we were often passed by Uncle Ken and Aunt Susie on their way to Eaton Corner to have Sunday dinner with Mabel and Mac. I had heard

Ken, Susie and Charles in Dew Drop Inn kitchen (Fraser family archives)

that they always took the food with them, which Aunt Susie had prepared ahead of time. (David Fraser)

I have fond memories of going into the store and Uncle Ken letting us choose candy which he put in little brown paper bags. He would also cut the top third off the cover of a bunch of Archie comic books and give them to us for free. Sometimes we'd go into the kitchen in the back of the store and chat with Auntie Susie. (Andrea Fraser)

My earliest memories, when I was around 10 years old: free comics with the tops cut off, ice cream, candies and the old drawer till. (Charles C. Fraser)

My memories were of picking out candies from the big glass candy jars and getting comic books with the covers half cut off! We would sit in the vinyl-seated booth and read the comics. Sometimes we went "into the back" to visit with Uncle Ken and Aunt Susie. (Elaine Fraser)

I remember Uncle Ken and Aunt Susie's warm smiles and how they made me feel so welcome. They always seemed so delighted when we'd pay them a visit. I also remember receiving marbles from Uncle Ken; I marvelled with delight at the wonder of their various sizes and designs. (Elizabeth Fraser Harvey)

On Sunday afternoons when Kevin was very young, he and I frequently visited Mom and Dad in Cookshire, and Kevin's great-grandmother at St. Paul's Home in Bury. After this, Kevin often asked me if we could stop at

Uncle Ken's. Sometimes I'd say that we really did not have enough time. But Kevin pleaded, "Mom, please, we'll stay only five minutes." I replied, "Kevin, it's impossible to go to Uncle Ken's for only five minutes." I always relented because Uncle Ken was fun, he said, and Kevin loved the treats and comic books that Uncle Ken gave him. Of course, I loved engaging in conversation with our dear uncle too. (Marilyn Fraser Reed)

Susie's cousin, Bobbie Bowen, who would become a frequent visitor, reflects on one of his early visits:

I didn't go up to Cookshire too often from Long Island (New York) until I got my driver's license. Then, very soon afterwards, I took my first solo trip to Cookshire when I was 16. I remember being up there in that front living room and Mabel playing the piano.

Time for friends and neighbours

In Ken and Susie's world, friends and neighbours were treated as though they were family. Several of them recount their early memories:

My earliest memories were at four or five years old, going in with my father and mother. (Christopher Standish)

What I remember most about Dew Drop Inn was studying for June exams on Ken and Susie's upstairs porch while listening to the customers below. (Rodger Heatherington)

When I lived in Bishopton, on Sundays my parents would take me with them when they went visiting friends and relatives around the area. When we went through Cookshire, my father would always stop at the Dew Drop Inn to chat with Uncle Ken. That was always the highlight for me. Uncle Ken would call me Little Princess, and let me spend time looking around the store. Then as we'd be leaving, he'd always give me a little brown bag filled with either gumdrops, jellybeans or those big white peppermints. (Marilyn Mackenzie Fraser, from the Christmas 1994 issue of the Fraser Family Link)

My first memories of the Dew Drop Inn were in 1939 when I was staying with the Rev. Carr's family for Christmas, and we would go to the Dew Drop Inn to meet other people. I remember how kind Susie and Ken were to a lost little English girl. I had come to Canada on a school trip from England with other girls from different schools in the Manchester area. We were on the ship on our way back home to England when the war broke out so we had to turn around and come back to Canada. I stayed in Canada throughout the war. (Joyce Standish)

In the early 1960s, several senior students from C.H.S. went to Dew Drop Inn regularly for the noon hour. I think they filled the two booths to play cards and talk with Uncle Ken and George Irving Willard, the East Angus school bus driver. (Marilyn Fraser Reed)

I remember that a lot of the kids from C.H.S. would go down there at noon or after school. (Bob Taylor)

When my husband, Bob, was teaching in Cookshire, he told me that the high school students would go to Dew Drop Inn to socialize and smoke. Ken would keep lookout and if a teacher approached, he would warn the students so they could quickly put out their cigarettes! (Muriel French Fitzsimmons)

Susie was always cheerful and they were both very kind to my two girls. We were neighbours for 18 years. Ken let them use one of his back sheds as a camp. (Almon Pope)

I spent a good deal of my youth between Pope's store and the Dew Drop Inn. It wasn't rare to go up his stairs to see a hand-painted sign in the door window that read, "Back in 5 minutes" or "Back in 15 minutes." I'd try the door anyway and sometimes it would open and Ken would come out of the kitchen and we'd visit. Many of these times he would be there and I still don't know whether this wasn't some sort of mischief on his part. The best sign I would see on occasion was "On the roof." It fooled me the first time that I saw it. I went back down the stairs and looked up before it dawned on me that it had to be a joke. If you saw the steepness of that tin roof and factored in Ken's age, there was no way he'd be up there! (Almon Pope)

I remember feeling a great friendship with Ken and Susie. I was always welcomed when I stopped in. Ken would always call me "Pope" and never used my first name. We would always visit over the counter and he would call Susie at some point ("Susie, Pope is here"). She would come out from the kitchen to greet me ("Hello, Pope") and then go back to whatever she was doing. My first job, other than working at Pope's store, was delivering the newspapers for Ken – The Sherbrooke Daily Record, Montreal Gazette and Star Weekly. I would get paid on Saturdays. The Star Weekly was a Saturday delivery whereas the others were weekdays. I had some good stories I would tell Ken about different encounters while delivering – one involving nudity and another encountering drunkenness. Ken delighted in hearing about these episodes as well as other on goings in my everyday life that I would recount to him as a trusted friend. When I had a good enough story, he would again call Susie ("Susie, come out here. Pope, tell her that story!"). Ken would always keep my grandfather's Sherbrooke Record and deliver it himself to the store without fail. Later on, I was again hired to work on Susie's house that had been bequeathed to her upon Johnny McInally's death. Ken didn't approve of the money she was paying out to fix the place up and they would argue somewhat over the issue. (Almon Pope)

Joyce and Donnie Standish first met at the Dew Drop Inn. (Charles W.K. Fraser)

I was on the skating rink but I couldn't skate and I was just standing there. Donnie was skating backwards and hit a bump and fell at my feet. That's how I first met him. (Joyce Standish)

I met my future husband, Donald Wright, at the Dew Drop Inn. His brothers, Hugh and Bob, were friends of Charles and visited there often. I didn't know how to serve gas, so I asked Don and *Voilà!* – that was the beginning of a 60-year friendship including 56 years of marriage. (Betty MacRae Wright)

Time for Church

St. Peter's Church and Dew Drop Inn, 1978 (Photo by Jim Fraser)

St. Peter's Anglican Church was located directly across the street from the Dew Drop Inn. This proximity fostered a close relationship between the Frasers and the Church's minister/priest. In addition, it facilitated Susie's active participation in Church activities. As for Ken, he regularly attended the Sunday service, but always waited until the final bell before dashing across the street to take his place in the backmost pew. Family, friends and a former priest of the parish share their memories of the Frasers' involvement in the life of the Church:

Ken made sure that everyone who came in knew that a new minister had arrived across the street. (Christopher Standish)

Ken kept a sharp eye on me. He might have said the following day, "Where did you go last night? What were you doing?" Yeah, he wasn't

A time for everything

afraid to ask. (Rev. Ron West)

I was a member of the St. Peter's Church choir with Aunt Susie for several years, from 1959 to 1964 approximately. She rarely, if ever, missed a Sunday. She, Joyce Standish and others, sat across from me and some other young girls including Carol Standish. (Marilyn Fraser Reed)

Here are two verses of a little poem that I wrote many years ago about the good folk of St. Peter's Church:
And dear Uncle Ken,
Just slightly late again
Why does he always wait until the last bell?
Must have had just one more small story to tell.

And the organist and choir,
Despite boring hymns they never did tire.
Aunt Susie, Dorothy Ross, Sister Marilyn, Joyce Standish
But those orange gowns and funny hats, how outlandish!
(Jim Fraser, from the Fraser Family Link, Christmas 2001)

Just in time for Church (Sketch by James Harvey)

> One time, I went over and the store was closed. The sign said "Back in 10 minutes." So I wandered around to the side door. When I knocked, Ken greeted me with "If you were coming, why didn't you phone first?" That's what he said, by way of joke really, as we had a good relationship. (Rev. Ron West)
>
> Susie was a member of the St. Peter's Choir. I remember her walking across the street from her place dressed in her choir gown. (Muriel Watson)
>
> I was in the choir for a while and remembered Susie there also. (Dorothy Shelton Dionne)
>
> Susie was a good and faithful churchgoer and was always making something for the sales table at Church sales. She was a wonderful singer in the choir. I have been a member of the choir from 1938 until now. (Dorothy Ross) *(Author's note: If my arithmetic is correct, Dorothy has sung in St. Peter's choir for 80 years!)*
>
> Susie often left her shop to give her time to sing at funerals, etc. (Betty MacRae Wright)
>
> I recall polishing Church brass with many older ladies of the church. It always needed more polishing, although to a child it seemed quite brilliant to begin with. (Dr. Emily Hamilton)
>
> I remember Ken would always pay his respects at the many funeral parlour visits when we lost community members. He would always remove his cap when coming in. I was a pall bearer at Ken's funeral. (Almon Pope)

Susie was someone who was not shy about sharing her Christian faith with others. One such instance is recounted by a very close friend:

> Whenever I was feeling overwhelmed with work or schedule, Susie would always remind me that the good Lord would never give me tasks to do without giving me the ability to do them. I still think of this frequently today. (Rodger Heatherington)

Church life was not without its lighter moments. I remember my Mom telling the following story. One week, Rev. Bill Cole, a family friend who often helped out at the Inn, was the guest preacher at St. Peter's. Bill didn't approve of smoking or drinking. In fact, when he worked in the Dew Drop, he refused to sell tobacco because he couldn't touch it with his hands. If he did so, he would be tainted for life. So, on this particular Sunday that he was to deliver the sermon, Ken filled Bill's jacket pockets with cigarettes. When Bill reached into his pocket for his sermon notes, he pulled out a handful of cigarettes! The story ends there, so it remains unknown whether the good Lord struck Bill dead for having touched the forbidden leaf!

A time for everything

Time for talking

Ken Fraser was a man of many words – all of them interesting and entertaining. He had a penchant for telling stories and his vocabulary was colourful, to say the least. Many of his expressions were unique. People share their memories of this talkative tale teller:

> Ken always had a story. His favourite expression was "Jiminy Cricket." (Christopher Standish)
>
> His enjoyment in storytelling was unforgettable, as he chewed on a toothpick and followed you to the door and then to the car, with one story after another! (David Fraser)
>
> Ken had a knack for turning a small incident into a huge saga. (Betty MacRae Wright)
>
> I recall the many memorable and thought-provoking discussions on such a wide assortment of subjects, but especially politics. (Steve Fraser)
>
> A five minute stop was always at least a half hour as Uncle Ken had another story to tell. (Marina Fraser Tracy, from the Christmas 1994 issue of the Fraser Family Link)
>
> What fun we had there! I remember the people that Ken was always teasing. He especially loved teasing the girls. (Louise Knox)
>
> Ken was a character! (Elizabeth Hurd Richardson)
>
> I remember dropping in sometimes for five minutes and still being there an hour later. You just never realized how long you'd been there because you were never bored. (Diane Fraser Keet)
>
> He used to tell us kids that he could "bite an inch off a nail", and when he finally showed us how, many months (or years) later, I was quite disappointed. (He held the nail an inch or so from his mouth and then he bit into the air – which was an inch away from the nail, or "off" the nail.). I can remember him telling Pierre Demers and me that there were two kinds of "good" people: those who were good and those who were good for nothing! One of his favourite expressions was "by golly." (David Fraser)
>
> At the end of many long chats, I wanted to say, "Well, I must be going" but he would stop me after "well" and say, "Not very well, and you?" or "Quite well, and you?" (Warren Fraser)
>
> Some of his frequent expressions: "Oh, I'm tellin' you!" "Here's the kicker…" "Here's the payoff…" (Jim Fraser)
>
> I would ask Ken how he was, and he would say that he'd been able to take a little nourishment. So, I guess that meant that he was okay. (Dorothy Shelton Dionne)

Ken never worried that his expressions or actions might sometimes be more appropriate for the locker room than for a public place like a general store. Therefore sometimes his comments tended to be crass or downright crude. Family and close friends recall such instances.

> Ken's favorite expressions were sometimes unprintable. (Joyce Standish)

> He would often cuss and use odd phrases such as "bald headed fart." (Greg Fraser)

> One time I recall Uncle Ken farting very loudly in the presence of customers and remarking, "Mange des bins, je pense." (Jim Fraser)

> Before I came to study for the priesthood, I was a sailor, also a miner for 28 years, so I was never shocked by Ken's sometimes colourful language. (Rev. Ron West)

> I remember as a paperboy for Ken, one Saturday, completely out of the blue he asks me, "Pope, do you have a girlfriend yet?" I replied something like, "Not at this time." and Ken says, "Well, one day you'll get a little of that stuff on your fingers and you'll never be the same." I didn't have the foggiest idea of what the hell he meant at the time. He could be very spontaneous in some of his remarks. (Almon Pope)

Personally, I remember a somewhat similar incident that happened to me when I was probably only about 10 years old. One day, as I entered the Dew Drop, Uncle Ken asked me "Did you hear about Mr. Smith?" When I replied "No." he continued, "Well, he had an operation yesterday and now he's only half a man." I didn't have the faintest idea what he was talking about. All I could think of was that poor Mr. Smith had been sawed in two, or at the very least, had had half his internal organs removed! In retrospect, I assume that Mr. Smith perhaps had had a testiculectomy, but at the time as a naïve young kid, I was totally in the dark.

Although Ken detested politicians and politics per se, he never shied away from political conversation.

> Ken loved talking politics and he was very opinionated. I remember one particular day an American fellow came in just to browse around and Ken got into talking politics with him. It ended up that the fellow got upset and headed for the door and opened it to the point that the bell rang and Ken said, "Oh, c'mon back now." The fellow shut the door and they resumed a conversation that again turned to politics and sure enough the guy headed for the door again and that bell rang a second time. Ken apologized to him and, sure enough, the guy returned once more. This time, Ken started talking about trains but before long he got back into politics and the fellow got really mad and the bell rang for the last time. I was in awe at how he kept baiting the guy. It left me with the impression that Ken wasn't terribly fond of Americans or at least not this American. (Almon Pope)

A time for everything

Ken had no use for politicians. One day, a guy comes in to the Dew Drop and says "Are you Mr. Fraser?" Ken says "Yes, and who are you?" The guy says "I'm running for such and such position. . ." Ken cuts him off with "The only position I like for a politician to be in is the horizontal position!" and the guy makes a hasty exit. (Bobbie Bowen)

Ken used to tell a little story about Pierre Trudeau riding around Montreal on a motorcycle during the war. (Barbara Keys Lassenba)

Ken could always be counted on to tell everyone the latest news – whether it was about the previous night's local fire or flood or the latest breaking world news.

I remember that whenever Dad came to Cookshire, pretty quickly he decided to go to Ken's in order to catch up on local news. My dad was Lawrence Belford, the son of Hulbert O. N. Belford, minister of the Anglican Church in Cookshire for several years. (Barbara Challies)

June 28, 1959: . . . heavy rain and storm. Lights off soon after church started. Storm very bad. Ours and cellars had water in them. Flooding at St. Cyr's, the hotel, Goff's and the Woollen Mill. Foundation of Ord's washed away. Debris all over the tracks. (Mabel Fraser's diary)

February 26, 1960. At 4:30 a.m. the fire siren blew, Turcotte's garage had burned down. (Mabel Fraser's diary)

Left: Ord house foundation washed away in flood , 1959 (Photo by author)
Right: Turcotte garage fire, 1960 (Photo by author)

I think it was from Uncle Ken that we first heard of the assassination of JFK. (Diane Fraser Keet)

I heard about the JFK assassination at the Dew Drop Inn when having a drink after school. (Christopher Standish)

JFK assassination headline (www.themontrealgazette.com)

Ken would often say, "Did you know such and such a person that passed away," often before it was in the Record newspaper. (Dorothy Shelton Dionne)

In addition to telling stories, berating politicians and spreading news, Ken also was known on occasion to impart morsels of timeless wisdom:

I remember Mr. Fraser telling me one early evening after I had had a long day of work, "Son, I've lived a long life and never have I heard a man say on his death bed 'I should have spent more time at the office.'" (Pierre Ellyson)

Time for celebrating

Mabel Fraser – Mac McVetty wedding, 1960 (Courtesy of Louise Knox)

Charles Fraser – Myrna Savage wedding, 1957 (Fraser family archives)

The Frasers always took time to celebrate special occasions involving family or friends. Among these were the weddings of their two children, Mabel and Charles, and their own 60th Wedding Anniversary. No doubt there were scores of other similar events. For example, when our first child was born, Uncle Ken and Aunt Susie marked the occasion by sending us a beautiful congratulatory card.

Ken and Susie celebrating their 60th Wedding Anniversary with Charles and Myrna, 1988 (Photo by author)

Ken and Susie with grand-niece Elaine Fraser (Photo by author)

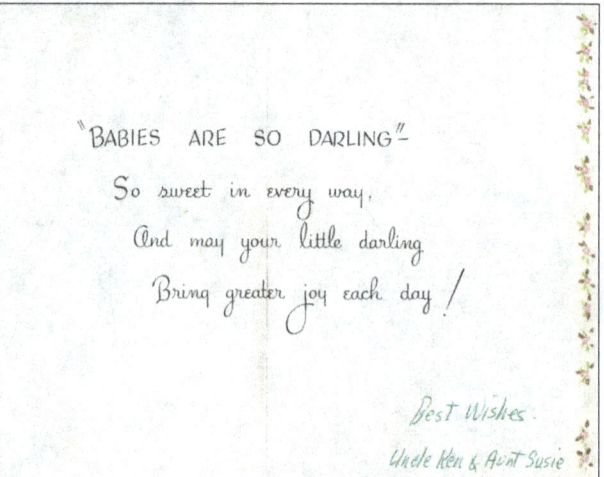

Andrea Fraser baby card from Ken and Susie, 1968 (Fraser family archives)

Card of Thanks

FRASER — We would like to thank all our family and friends for the wonderful 60th wedding anniversary party they gave us on the afternoon of November 19, 1988 in St. Peter's Church Hall, Cookshire, where over 350 well-wishers attended from far and near. A special thank you to our son and wife, Charles and Myrna, of Prescott, Ontario, also Myrna's sister Brenda and husband Robert Harrison of Brockville, Ontario, to our nieces and nephews and especially to Malcolm Fraser who helped so much and in so many ways (to organize this great get-together), and to the Ladies Guild of St. Peter's who served the delicious lunch and refreshments. Also, many thanks to all those dear friends who sent such lovely cards, currency and gifts, also bouquets of beautiful roses, plants, etc. and the lovely 3-tiered anniversary cake that was supplied by Myrna and Charles. We wish to express our sincere thanks and appreciation to all others who helped in any way to make our 60th anniversary such a memorable occasion. Your thoughtfulness and best wishes will be long remembered. A sincere thank you to one and all.
KEN & SUSIE FRASER
Cookshire

Card of Thanks clipping from The Record (Fraser family archives)

Time for grieving

Unfortunately, life is also marked by very sad moments such as the passing of loved ones. Particularly devastating to Ken and Susie was the death of their daughter Mabel in 1981 at the young age of 52. Being an ever-present member of the Dew Drop Inn family both before and after

MCVETTY, Mabel Fraser — In loving memory of our dear daughter, sister and aunt who departed this life 11 years ago, March 20, 1981.
A silent thought, a silent tear
And a constant wish that you were here.
No need for words except to say
Still loved, still missed in every way.
MOM and DAD
CHARLES, MYRA & FAMILY

Mabel In Memoriam clipping from The Record (Fraser family archives)

A time for everything

her marriage to Malcolm "Mac" McVetty, her passing left a big hole. In a letter to niece June Fraser Patterson shortly afterwards, Ken writes:

> Dear June, Gordon and family,
>
> Thought I'd drop you a few lines tonight along with card. I had been thinking of phoning you several times lately on weekends. . . . We want to thank you from deep down in our hearts for being so kind and thoughtful to us . . . believe me it's still awful lonesome around here sometimes. . . . Guess I'll have to say so long for this time . . .
>
> Love from Uncle Ken and Aunt Susie. (June Fraser Patterson)

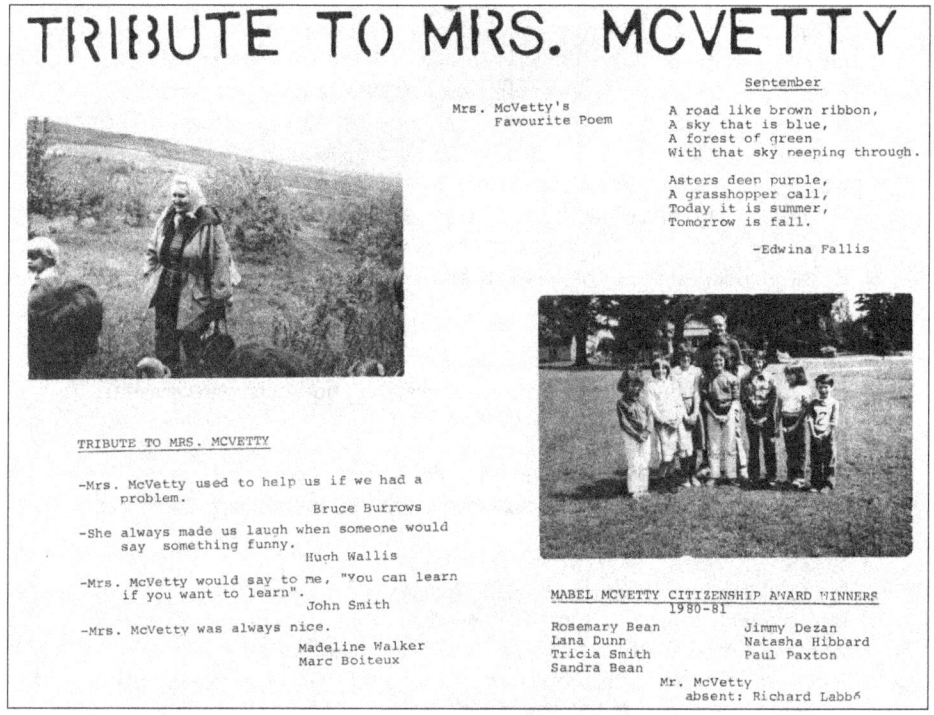

Ayer's Cliff School tribute to Mabel Fraser McVetty (Fraser family archives)

Time for giving

One of the most popular adjectives ascribed by family and friends to both Ken and Susie was "generous." And that generosity was shown in countless ways from simple gestures to significant gifts. A few of them are documented here:

> When I was a young boy Ken always gave me a peppermint. (Christopher Standish)

We'd go in to buy ice cream and he'd give us candies as a bonus. (Bob Taylor)

From mid-1951 to mid-1956, I worked at the post office for John McKenna. A little while after I began, when I was only 11 years old, Pat Maurice filed a complaint that I was too young to be working there and they stepped in and I lost my job until I became 12 years old in January 1952. My hours were 5 a.m. to 9 a.m. and 4 p.m. to 8 p.m. Monday to Friday, and 5:00 a.m. to 1 p.m. on Saturday. When Susie found this out she had Ken arrange with John McKenna that I take my break from 8:45 a.m. to 9 o'clock. And so, I would stop at the Dew Drop Inn for breakfast. And again, school got out at 3:30 p.m., I'd stop there for supper on the way to work.

I never paid a cent for those meals. However, I worked it off restocking for Ken and minding the store on Sundays while they went to church or sometimes on a Sunday afternoon outing. And later, on weekends, so the family could go to the States (Claremont, New Hampshire) to visit and shop, as both Mabel and Susie were shopaholics. My helping out was a give and take kind of situation as things were very difficult at home. Ken and Susie had helped arrange for my job at the post office when my parents had split up and things were pretty drastic financially. It was my salary from this work that was keeping my mother and me afloat. (Rodger Heatherington)

My most vivid memory was that Ken was always generous to my brother and me. He gave us many comic books, but not before removing a portion of the cover. (Neil Burns)

Uncle Ken used to give us candy and comic books with the top part of the front cover missing. Aunt Susie never forgot any of us at Christmas. (David Fraser)

My family didn't have a TV until 1957 so we went over to the Dew Drop Inn to watch programs such as Perry Como, Ed Sullivan, etc. Everyone was welcomed to their upstairs living room and we even got snacks. Susie's kitchen was open house for many young people including college students John and David Ward. At Christmas time the kitchen was crammed with people. (Betty MacRae Wright)

In 1958 I had turned 18. When home from Montreal one weekend I complained to Ken and Susie that my father was going to sell the cottage for $1000. I wanted to buy it, but my father didn't take me seriously and said I could never save the money. As my parents had been separated for over six years and I was the sole support for my mother as well as paying my own expenses in Montreal, I knew that he was probably right. One day during the week Ken called and said he had arranged a meeting with my father for Saturday evening. He told me that John McKenna would also be there and that he wanted me to be present. However, I wasn't to say anything – just agree with him no matter what. So we met. My father stated that his price was $1000 and that the first person to produce the cash would get the property. Ken said, "I thought you would say that" and laid $1000 in hundred dollar bills on the table. When my father then tried to raise the price, Ken said, "No, you made an offer and John and Rodger witnessed it." I paid Ken back over the next year and he wouldn't consider taking any interest. Ken and Susie were both closer to me and my upbringing than my own parents. They were the finest and most moral people you could ever hope to meet. (Rodger Heatherington)

March 16, 1959: Ronnie Langworth spent the night here as Daddy couldn't get him home (*due to a bad snowstorm*) (Mabel Fraser's diary)

Elsewhere in this book you have read about many other examples of Fraser generosity. It was part of Ken and Susie's modus operandi. It is not surprising then to learn that Ken passed away without having collected all outstanding bills. Son Charles explains:

There was money on the books when Dad passed away. People still owed him money. Yes, Dad was generous but he was also thrifty. He was an awful fellow for not paying a bill before it was due. He was happy to pay it but only when it was due. He thought that to pay it sooner was a waste of money. Mom was just the opposite. She paid the bill the day she got it!

Dew Drop Inn

Chapter 12   In the last days

Painting of Dew Drop Inn by Joe Beaulieu (Courtesy of Pierre Ellyson and Roger Dionne)

The decline

The Dew Drop Inn's last days were preceded by a long period of decline. Its demise in 1994 was not a case of sudden death. Rather, it succumbed to a progressive deterioration in health that began decades earlier. Various components of the once-booming Dew Drop Inn enterprise gradually declined and disappeared. First to go was the inn business itself, which dropped off earlier then effectively ended in the late 1950s. Because it was the flagship portion of the entire Dew Drop Inn business, this was a severe setback. Additional shrinkage occurred in the decades that followed. In the mid-1970s, the gas station appendage would be amputated. Meanwhile, the restaurant business had literally gone to the dogs. That left only the general store. And it too had its challenges. As mentioned in an earlier chapter, it was forced to make major changes to its signage in order to comply with Quebec's language laws.

Dew Drop Inn sign modified to conform to Quebec language laws (Fraser family archives; enhanced by G. Beck)

At the same time as business within its weathered walls was declining, the Dew Drop Inn building itself was suffering from a severe lack of maintenance – both inside and out. Ken was getting on in years and had neither the muscle nor the motivation that he once had. In many ways, it is quite astonishing that he was able to keep the place going as long as he did.

Dew Drop Inn closing garage sale, 1994 (Photo by René Bolduc)

Anticipating the inevitable, Jane George, writing in the Globe and Mail of April 11, 1992, penned:

In the last days

> We try not to think about all kinds of things, like the day, probably not too far off, when Cookshire's Dew Drop Inn finally closes. For more than 60 years the Frasers have run this store in a weathered clapboard building down Main Street. Inside, glass jars still overflow with vanilla creams and peppermints, and Kenneth Fraser sits behind the curving wooden counter surrounded by vintage merchandise and memories from more than 80 years in Cookshire. I didn't go to the Dew Drop Inn too often this winter, so that when it's gone I will hurt less.

In retrospect, it is quite clear that the writing was on the wall. The Dew Drop Inn's days were numbered. But the final death knell was not sounded until December 1993 when Ken passed away. Even so, the building would survive almost another full year. During that grace period, there were some who wanted to see the place preserved for its historical significance.

On March 31, 1994, an article appeared in the Journal Le Haut-Saint-François newspaper entitled "The Haut-Saint-François Historical and Heritage Society wishes that our old houses would be spared from demolition." The following text has been excerpted (and translated from French):

> Too often, when a house gets old, whether it is of a particular style or is typical of its period, it either gets demolished or is assigned a new use that is totally inconsistent with its original vocation. . . . It is impossible to recreate a demolished house . . . In the town of Cookshire there is a house that was built around 1850. Our Society ardently hopes that someone will offer to acquire the house and restore it to its original condition thus allowing it to continue its vocation as a beacon of our town's business and residential history . . . There is no time to lose. Once its ruins litter the ground, it will be too late to be sorry that that we failed to take the initiative to save Cookshire's Dew Drop Inn.

But alas, no one heeded the Historical and Heritage Society's plea. Perhaps potentially interested parties, if indeed there were any, realized that the building was beyond saving. In any case, the Dew Drop Inn's destiny was clear – demolition. But before the wrecker's ball would arrive, there would be a multi-month garage sale.

Jane George, in a very touching Globe and Mail article entitled "Farewell to the Dew Drop Inn" that was published April 9, 1994, wrote:

> The neon *Vendu* sticker over the realtor's sign means the Dew Drop Inn has finally been sold. . . The store's entire merchandise is being sold in a seemingly endless garage sale. . . Last week, it took all my courage to walk back into the store to see the sale and say hello. I bought a few boxes of greeting cards, a box of ancient soap, and a balsam-wood canoe paddle fancifully etched for tourists with "Cookshire, Que."

Dew Drop Inn for sale, 1994 (Photo by Almon Pope)

The demise

The Christmas 1994 issue of the Fraser Family Link published the death notice opposite:

> "INN, DEW DROP. Suddenly, at Cookshire, Quebec, on November 21, 1994 at the age of approx. 100 after several years of failing health. Beloved home of Susie and the late Ken Fraser. Fondly remembered by family, friends and passers-by."

On an appropriately cold and dreary day, November 21, 1994, the elderly structure breathed its last breath. A headline and captioned photo in the December 1, 1994 issue of Journal Le Haut-Saint-François reported this final moment in the life of the Dew Drop Inn:

> The Dew Drop Inn is no more. The recent demolition of the Dew Drop Inn building in Cookshire marks the disappearance of a relic of another era. This general store type establishment had a distinctive character. One had only to step inside to get the impression of going back in time. The enveloping atmosphere allowed one to experience the times of long

In the last days

Pharmacie Proxim's parking lot is the former Dew Drop Inn site (Photo by author)

ago. It took mere minutes for the heavy equipment to reduce the age-wearied structure to a pile of rubble.

In an article in the December 2008 issue of the Fraser Family Link, Jim Fraser commented on the building's final fate. "The Dew Drop Inn was demolished to make room for a parking lot. It was an ignominious end for this once-proud Cookshire institution."

The mementos

Some Dew Drop Inn mementos, clockwise from top left: Vase (Marilyn Fraser Reed); gumball dispenser (Kerri Fraser); peanut jar (Greg Fraser); Hunting's Dairy milk bottle (Christopher Standish); Frasier, Thornton & Co. Muskalene jar (Kerri Fraser); Bryant's crate (Greg Fraser)

Before the Dew Drop Inn building was brutally bulldozed, some significant pieces were salvaged. Included among the surviving artifacts were important parts of the store's display equipment, various pieces of furniture and dozens of miscellaneous items. Some of them have taken on new vocations in their custodian's home or place of business. Others simply decorate their new owner's abodes or are lovingly tucked away for safekeeping. Whatever their destiny, they will forever rekindle fond memories of a place that once was, but is no longer.

Dew Drop Inn memento photograph "Unveiling Cookshire Soldiers' Monument, Nov. 11, 1920" (Courtesy of Christopher Standish)

Family and friends relate the parts they played in preserving the memories of Dew Drop Inn while others share their feelings of loss:

> I have the Dew Drop Inn's large showcase as well as the front counter that Ken stood behind. They are both installed in my business office, where the display case houses some of my own antique collection and the counter serves as my order counter. (Christopher Standish)

> The white kitchen hutch that I now have is the one that was in the Dew Drop Inn kitchen for many years. Gramp had cut the legs off because the floor was uneven. Somehow, we managed to find them and re-attach them. And I gave it a little paint to perk it up. The kitchen clock is something that most people will recognize, as it hung in the kitchen for as long as I can remember. I also have the furnace hot-air register grate from the store front – the one that was right in front of the comic books where people would stand to pay. It is now part of a custom-built coffee table in my living room. (Kerri Fraser)

> When they were clearing out before closing completely, I bought a few boxes of cards, kept them for special folks who knew the Dew Drop or had connections with it. This year I had only one card left. It was yellowed and aged but I sent it to the perfect person – our cousin Charles. I know he appreciated it. (June Fraser Patterson)

> I bought some old postcards of Dew Drop Inn when they were selling out. (Elizabeth Hurd Richardson)

Dew Drop Inn counter (top) and showcase recycled at Standish Distribution (Photos by author)

Dew Drop Inn memento Kitchen clock (above) and kitchen hutch (Photos by Kerri Fraser)

I grew up in Bury and one of the highlights of my childhood was going to Cookshire so that I could buy Archie comics and a small sweet treat at the Dew Drop Inn. It was always an extremely fun trip. I am now 47 years old and living in Cookshire. Whenever I walk by the spot where the store used to be, I fondly remember the many times I went into the store and I miss it. (Tracie Dougherty)

The Frasers were an integral part of the community and represented a way of life that has since, unfortunately, disappeared. (Rev. John Thevenot)

RIP Ken and Susie

As much as the different Dew Drop Inn mementos are treasured, they pale in comparison with the memories of Ken and Susie that are held so dearly. How do we remember them? Let us look at some of the ways.

Although almost a quarter century has passed since Ken left us, we can still see him standing behind the cluttered counter cajoling customers, sitting on a Bryant's Bull's Head ginger ale box lettering Lister's lorry, donning his taxi driver's cap for his school bus run to "The Colony," sprinting across the street to St. Peter's or enjoying card games with his countless cribbage cronies.

Our memories of Susie, who passed away in 2004, are even fresher in our minds. We can see her scurrying about in perpetual motion, moving from one task to another. Dressed in her prim white uniform, we can see her giving someone a perm, cooking an apple pie or completing yet another afghan. Or dressed in

In the last days

Ken and Susie on their 60th Wedding Anniversary, 1988 (Photo by author, enhanced by G. Beck)

farmer's overalls and rubber boots, we can see her hiking up the hill to apply "shitilizer" to her garden. And on Sundays we can still see her in her choir gown as she adds her beautiful voice to the other St. Peter's choristers.

Yes, we nostalgically recall the many things that Ken and Susie achieved during their long and productive lives. But we remember with even greater appreciation who they were as people. As parents, they raised two

Death

FRASER, Kenneth — At the Sherbrooke Hospital on Tuesday, December 21, 1993, Kenneth Fraser in his 89th year. Beloved husband of Susan McGuire. Dear father of Charles (Myrna) and the late Mabel. Cherished grandfather of Joel, Gregory, Lori, Kerri, as well as 7 great-grandchildren. Resting at Cass Funeral Home, 50 Craig St. S., Cookshire, Que., where friends may call on Wednesday from 2 to 4 and 7 to 9 p.m. Funeral service will be held at St. Peter's Church, Cookshire, on Thursday, December 23, 1993 at 2 p.m., Canon Ronald West officiating. Interment in Cookshire Cemetery.

DEATHS

FRASER, Susan (Susie)
Peacefully at the Grace Christian Home, Lennoxville, Quebec on Tuesday, August 31st, 2004 in her 97th year. Susie Elizabeth McGuire. Beloved wife of the late Kenneth Fraser and dear mother of Charles (Myrna Savage) and the late Mabel. Cherished grandmother of Joel, Gregory (Sue), Lori (John Lamere) and Kerri as well as seven great-grandchildren. She is also survived by her brother John and sister Pearl Henderson.
Resting at the Cass Funeral Home, 6 Belvidere Road, Lennoxville, Quebec where family and friends may visit on Friday, September 3rd, 2004 from 2 to 4 and 7 to 9 p.m., and on Saturday, September 4th from 1 to 2 p.m. followed by the Funeral Service at 2 p.m. Rev. Canon Ron West officiating. Interment in the Cookshire Protestant Cemetery. As memorial tributes, donations to the Grace Christian Home, 1501 Campbell Avenue, Lennoxville, Quebec J1M 2A3, would be greatly appreciated by the family.

Ken and Susie death notices
(Ken: Sherbrooke Record /Fraser family archives; Susie: Brockville Recorder and Times /courtesy of Brockville Public Library)

fine children who both went on to have successful careers. They were loving grandparents who treated their grandkids to fun times and favourite foods. They were a beloved Auntie and Uncle to scores of nieces and nephews, all of whom they remembered with gifts at Christmas. And they were friends to many – all of whose lives they touched. They were the kind of friends who gave and gave, without asking anything in return. Neighbour Betty MacRae Wright remembers that "they kept an eye out for anyone who needed help."

Ken and Susie were special people indeed and we are all richer for having known them.

Ken and Susie's gravestone, Cookshire Cemetery (Photo by author)

Epilogue

In reading this book, you may have been puzzled by the chapter titles. Perhaps you considered some of them to be quite archaic or others to be somewhat irrelevant to the material covered in the chapter. But on the other hand, you might have detected a subtle consistency among them. In fact, each of the section titles consists of a phrase that can be found in a Bible verse. This was not a coincidence. It was done intentionally as a tribute to Ken and Susie Fraser's Christian faith and service. As mentioned in the book, not only were they faithful members and supporters of St. Peter's Anglican Church in Cookshire, but in living their lives, they consistently manifested the Christian qualities of hospitality, love, compassion and generosity.

The Bible references are as follows (from the New International Version unless specified otherwise):

Chapter 1 – In the beginning (Genesis 1:1)
Chapter 2 – Room at the inn (Luke 2:7)
Chapter 3 – Eat, drink and be merry (Luke 12:19)
Chapter 4 – All kinds of goods (Nehemiah 13:20)
Chapter 5 – Signs and wonders (Acts 5:12)
Chapter 6 – In the upper room (Acts 20:8 – English Standard Version)
Chapter 7 – Ride in his chariot (2 Kings 10:16 – King James Version)
Chapter 8 – From evening till morning (Exodus 27:21)
Chapter 9 – The fruit of her hands (Proverbs 31:31 – King James version)
Chapter 10 – The rumble of wheels (Nahum 3:2 – New Living Translation)
Chapter 11 – A time for everything (Ecclesiastes 3:1)
Chapter 12 – In the last days (Acts 2:17)
Appendix – It is written (Matthew 4:4)

In closing, we borrow from the Bible some parting words that are very applicable to the lives of Ken and Susie: "Well done, good and faithful servants." (Matthew 25:23) and "I have fought the good fight, I have finished the race, I have kept the faith." (2 Timothy 4:7). May Saint Peter's personal barber and principal sign painter rest in peace.

Ken and Susie helping Saint Peter (Sketch by James Harvey)

Appendix – It is written

This appendix contains reproductions of the following published articles referred to in this book:

- Anon., "Cookshire Nestles Peacefully Amid Picturesque Surroundings," *unknown newspaper*, February 25, 1933.

- Anon.,"Mr. and Mrs. Kenneth Fraser honored on their 60th wedding anniversary," *The Record* [Sherbrooke], 1988.

- Jane George, "Tough Times in the Townships," *The Globe and Mail* [Toronto], April 11, 1992.

- Anon., "Obituaries: Kenneth Ira Fraser ," *The Record* [Sherbrooke], January 19, 1994.

- Anon., "La Société d'histoire et du patrimoine du Haut-Saint-François souhaite que nos vielles maisons échappent au pic des démolisseurs" [The Haut-Saint-François Historical and Heritage Society wishes that our old houses would be spared from demolition], *Journal Le Haut-Saint-François* [Cookshire-Eaton], March 31, 1994.

- Jane George, "Farewell to the Dew Drop Inn," *The Globe and Mail* [Toronto], April 9, 1994.

- Claude Leclerc, "Cookshire: l'ancienne gare n'est plus" [The Cookshire Station is no more], *Journal Le Haut-Saint-François* [Cookshire-Eaton], October 27, 1994.

- Jean Murray Chute, "Memories of Dew Drop Inn," *Brome County News* [Lac-Brome], November 2, 1994.

- Anon., "Cookshire: Le Dew Drop Inn n'est plus" [The Dew Drop Inn is no more], *Journal Le Haut-Saint-François* [Cookshire-Eaton], December 1, 1994.

- Claudia Villemaire, "Cookshire Fair – 65th straight year for Cookshire veteran," *The Record* [Sherbrooke], August 17, 2000.

PAGE THIRTY

COOKSHIRE NESTLES PEACEFULLY AMID PICTURESQUE SURROUNDINGS

Chef Lieu of Compton County Is a Place of Natural Charm and Pleasant People—Surrounding Countryside Has Attracted Many Favorable Comments from Tourists and Visitors.

Feb. 25, 1933

John Levi, Luther French, Jesse Cooper, Abner Osgood, Orsemus and Ward Bailey, Ebenezer Learned and Captain John Cook are names which will ever remain closely associated with the early history of Cookshire. It was, in fact, from John Cook that the village received its name.

The first settlement of what is now the village of Cookshire dates back to the year 1797. The first settler on or near the site of the village was Israel Bailey, in 1798. Previous to the year 1892 the town formed part of the Township of Eaton, but in that year it was incorporated by an act of the Provincial Legislature and launched upon its triumphant journey to the status of an attractive and picturesque village, where peace and plenty make it an ideal place in which to live.

Until the building of the old International Railway line in 1870, the construction of which was largely due to the efforts of the late Hon. John Henry Pope, settlement was slow, but from 1870 onwards there was a marked increase. In 1886 the International Railway Company was acquired by the Atlantic and Northwest Railway Company, which in turn was leased to the Canadian Pacific Railway Company. This road now forms a link of the Canadian Pacific Railway's line between Montreal and Halifax, with a large passenger and freight service.

In 1887 the first work on the Hereford Railway was begun. During the winter of 1887 upwards of three hundred men were employed chopping out a right of way and piling up the cordwood for about twenty-five miles between Cookshire and the boundary line in Hereford. During the summer from 1,000 to 1,200 men were employed. After considerable difficulty the line was completed on January 6, 1889.

In 1892 Cookshire was erected into a separate municiaplity and was made the chef lieu of Compton County. The village is located on the many line from Montreal, it is twenty-two miles east of Sherbrooke and 121 miles from Montreal and the same distance from Quebec City.

Cookshire is built on the western slope of the valley of the Eaton River, and commands a fine view of one of the most picturesque sections of the Province of Quebec. One of the most popular highways leading from the New England States into the province and on the Quebec City passes through the village and affords the tourists glimpses of water and landscape views of rare charm and beauty.

Mr. and Mrs. Kenneth Fraser honored on their 60th wedding anniversary

On November 19, 1988, a very delightful afternoon was spent at St. Peter's Church Hall in Cookshire when friends and relatives gathered to honor Ken and Susie Fraser who were celebrating their 60th wedding anniversary.

They received a citation from the Prime Minister, Brian Mulroney. They were presented with a beautiful plaque from the congregation of St. Peter's for their years of dedication to the life of the church. The presentation was made by Malcolm Fraser who thanked the couple for their constant help. He noted the "far-reaching" effect of Ken's signs, announcing a recent Guild tea. Folks from Quebec City, "just passing thru'", saw the sign and stopped to enjoy the great hospitality of the St. Peter's ladies.

Marina Tracy, on behalf of the Fraser nephews and nieces, presented uncle Ken and aunt Susie with a framed photograph of a train as it left Cookshire chugging up the grade past the Fraser farm. The photography was by Winston Fraser.

Charles brought greetings to his mom and dad from him and Myrna, children and grandchildren. He was so pleased that everyone came to help his parents celebrate.

The happy couple thanked everyone for coming and for the many beautiful gifts and cards, as well as a 3-tiered anniversary cake furnished by Myrna and Charles.

While the guests had a grand time chatting with the bride and groom of 60 years, and visiting with each other, the ladies of St. Peter's Guild kept the buffet table filled with delicious refreshments.

Guests and relatives were present from Prescott, Kingston and Ottawa, Ontario, and throughout the Townships.

It was a special treat to have relatives from Claremont and Newport, New Hampshire — Thelma McGuire, Jimmy McGuire, his wife and her mother and Mrs. Paquette.

Two great-grandchildren, Jennifer and Ashley, children of Greg and Susan, from Kingston, Ont., added greatly to the joy of the occasion.

"Every anniversary with our Father as a guide-
Is certain to be blessed when two hearts share it...
Side by side."

May Ken and Susie have many more happy years together.

LETTER FROM QUEBEC / *It has not been a good year in the Eastern Townships. Factories have closed, friends have left for Toronto and Calgary. But the English-speaking community still has its ties*

Tough times in the Townships

BY JANE GYORGY

ON this evening walk after a brilliant but cold spring day we're following an immense, almost tropical sun. But, before we can fully appreciate it, the sun disappears behind the spiky ridge of trees.

Our conversation tonight revolves around a difficult year. Over all, it has been 12 months of losses here in the Eastern Townships. My two hands are not enough to count the friends who no longer have work. Cookshire's trailer factory, which burned down spectacularly last February, will not be rebuilt, and these days the town's plastics shop is down to about 40 workers from more than 300. The employees went on strike in the autumn for better conditions. Now, the company is putting its energy elsewhere and leaving our contentious citizenry to their own resources.

It's been a year of personal loss, too, as a whole generation walked through the obituaries: my husband's grandmother, both parents, two uncles, a cousin and two close friends died. Our family gatherings are spooky affairs now, with more empty chairs than faces as we doggedly celebrate holidays, anniversaries and even birthdays (Uncle Jack would have been 89 on Christmas Eve) of those passed on.

It's been a winter for solitary reflection, but, now that the roads are free of snow, the Unity Oddfellow Lodge in Sherbrooke held a chicken-pie supper. Perhaps 40 people came out. Many were familiar faces, others unknown, but with the rough, swollen hands from farm chores I recognize immediately. They are all the parents of friends already gone to Ottawa, Toronto or Calgary.

There's not an English-speaking person left in the Townships who hasn't asked themselves at least once whether they're leaving Quebec. Real-estate agents' signs in front of many homes show who has decided, although there is no hope of selling. We decide only to repaint our upstairs, erasing a decade of accumulated wood smoke from the kitchen stove. It's an agreeable cosmetic solution to our indecision: nicer to live in now, maybe a good investment later.

We try not to think about all kinds of things, like the day, probably not too far off, when the Cookshire's Dew Drop Inn finally closes. For more than 60 years the Frasers have run this store in a weathered clapboard building down Main Street. Inside, glass jars still overflow with vanilla creams and peppermints, and Kenneth Fraser sits behind the curving wooden counter surrounded by vintage merchandise and memories from more than 80 years in Cookshire. I didn't go to the Dew Drop Inn too often this winter, so that when it's gone I will hurt less.

This year the Townships lost its only English-language radio station. We still have our newspaper. It's the Sherbrooke Record, the sole English daily in Quebec outside Montreal and our source of local news for more than a century. Often this is in the form of "Social Notes" from villages no longer officially recognized on Quebec maps, but vital to our fragile collective psyche. We learn who has motored where, lunched with whom or received visitors from out of province in Maple Grove, Ditchfield, Island Brook or Mystic.

Equally important for information are the classifieds: garage sales, numerous as we put our affairs in order; auctions, more plentiful than ever, always exciting, if bittersweet; and last but not least, death notices telling us who has permanently left our diminished anglophone community. And in the Record's letters section those who are still kicking carry on their battles, personal, public and sometimes imagined.

"We're coming to the end of an era," I say, thinking about the past year, the Townships, for so long home, but often a lonely, insecure place today. "No, two eras — isn't an era 75 years?" says my husband, mulling over seven generations of his family history as we walk down the road out of Cookshire. The sky is tinged with the sun, now set. Across the valley, lights begin to flicker in the barns. The pinkish snow reminds me of confectioner's sugar over the sweetest, most beautiful countryside I know.

Jane Gyorgy is a writer-broadcaster living in Cookshire, Que.

It is written

Obituaries

KENNETH IRA FRASER
of Cookshire, Quebec

Kenneth Ira Fraser passed away at the Sherbrooke Hospital on Tuesday, December 21, 1993.

He was born in Cookshire on December 3, 1905, son of Charles Ira Fraser and his wife Lilla Joyce. He grew up on the family farm in Cookshire and graduated from Cookshire High School.

On November 28, 1928 he was united in marriage with Susan McGuire, who survives him. They started their married life in Sherbrooke where they resided for 1½ years, during which time Ken worked for the C.P.R. In May 1930, he purchased the Planche Millinery Store in his hometown of Cookshire. It was then that he started a restaurant business, which became known as the "Dew Drop Inn".

Over the years, he also became a well known sign painter and drove taxi as well as driving school children in his Hudson to school. He worked at this for 64 years, becoming a well known landmark to young and old alike.

On November 28, 1993, Susie and Ken celebrated their 65th Wedding Anniversary.

He was predeceased by his daughter Mabel in March of 1981. He leaves to mourn his loss his wife Susie and his son Charles (Myrna) of Prescott, Ontario, four grandchildren and seven great-grandchildren.

His remains rested at Cass Funeral Home, Cookshire, where relatives, neighbours and a host of friends paid their last respects. There were many beautiful floral arrangements and donations to St. Peter's Anglican Church which showed the esteem in which he was held.

The funeral service took place at St. Peter's Anglican Church, Cookshire, on December 23, 1993 at 2 p.m. The Rev. Canon Ron West officiated. The hymns sung by the choir, with Mrs. Roberta Smith as organist, were "Safe In the Arms Of Jesus" and "Mine Eyes Have Seen The Glory".

The bearers were Russell Nutbrown, Douglas Mackay, Malcolm Fraser, Rodger Heatherington, Almon Pope and Roland Warburton.

Burial will take place in Cookshire Cemetery in the Spring.

A lovely lunch was served after the funeral in St. Peter's Church Hall, to all family, relatives and friends, by the A.C.W.

Ken will be sadly missed by all his loved ones and friends. His dry wit and friendly conversation made him a friend to young and old alike.

La Société d'histoire et du patrimoine du Haut-Saint-François souhaite que nos vieilles maisons échappent au pic des démolisseurs

Les villes, les villages, même les plus modestes hameaux sont hérissés de maisons d'un autre âge, ce qui témoigne de leur vie passée. Ces constructions ont une vie. C'est dire que chacune a eu sa jeunesse et sa période de grande utilité.

Trop souvent, lorsqu'une maison vieillit, fut-elle d'un style particulier, image de sa période d'érection, on la démolit, sinon on l'affecte à des fins absolument incohérentes avec sa vocation d'origine. Quoi qu'il survienne, elle ne sera plus là pour témoigner du passé. C'est un peu comme si on détruisait les documents d'une municipalité après son centenaire parce que l'on croit que cette paperasse ne sera plus jamais utile. C'est presque comme si, sans dommage, sans regret, sans pincement de conscience, on pouvait abattre l'âme d'une personne quand son corps est assez développé! Bien oui, les vieilles maisons, même les vieux objets, ont une âme. Cette âme se reflète sur son entourage pour rappeler les origines du milieu. Les dommages sont irréparables. Il est impossible de recréer une maison démolie.

«Qu'on se hâte avant l'arrivée du pic des démolisseurs. Lorsque les ruines joncheront le sol, il sera trop tard pour regretter de ne pas avoir pris l'initiative de conserver le Dew Drop Inn de Cookshire», signale la Société d'histoire et du patrimoine du Haut Saint-François.

Pourtant, elle était là depuis longtemps, rappelant les premiers temps d'une ville, d'un village, à ceux qui aiment y vivre et qui la veulent belle et active et pour émouvoir les gens qui ont laissé le milieu.

Dans la ville de Cookshire, il existe une maison qui fut bâtie aux environs de 1850. Elle est la propriété de la Succession Kenneth Fraser. Le propriétaire de cette construction était le vieux Ken comme le nommaient bien amicalement nos concitoyens anglophones.

L'âge a terrassé M. Fraser il y a quelques semaines. Devant sa propriété. Depuis, on a installé l'affiche À vendre devant sa porte. Kenneth Fraser était un amoureux des vieilles choses et une mine de renseignements sur la petite histoire de la localité. Il habitait d'ailleurs le 30 de la rue Principale Ouest depuis 65 ans. Il y a empilé des montagnes de vieux objets, vieux livres et revues, sans compter certains de ses travaux personnels comme peintre en affichage.

Notre société souhaite ardemment que quelqu'un s'offre d'acquérir la maison pour la rénover, tout en lui conservant son cachet original, la laissant ainsi continuer sa vocation de point d'ancrage de l'histoire commerciale et résidentielle de notre ville.

It is written

THE GLOBE AND MAIL
CANADA'S NATIONAL NEWSPAPER
Saturday, April 9, 1994

LETTER FROM COOKSHIRE, QUEBEC / *It was a store straight out of the past: wooden stairs, ceiling-high shelves, a tinny bell over the door and an owner who spun tales*

Farewell to the Dew Drop Inn

BY JANE GYORGY

THE neon *Vendu* sticker over the realtor's sign means the Dew Drop Inn has finally been sold. And now people here say the faded yellow clapboard building will be torn down to make room for a parking lot.

Perhaps, then, I'll recall the image from a postcard taken of the Dew Drop as it was in the 1930s, with a cheerful line of parasols and a pair of spindly gas pumps out front. During its heyday, Cookshire's Dew Drop Inn was a popular way-station for travellers heading to and from the States. It was part service station, part lunch counter and part general store.

Those days were always fresh to Kenneth Fraser, owner of the Dew Drop Inn. For over 60 years, from year to year, he waited on odd passers-by. From generation to generation, he dispensed penny candy to the village children.

But over the last few years, enough people never seemed to stop by. Most English-speaking youngsters grew up and moved away. And drivers became hesitant to stop at the somewhat shabby store, with its French sign *Varietes* nailed on at an angle. So, inside, the gaudy boxes of Ganong chocolates languished in the cooler well after Valentine's Day, close by a piece of cake saved from Kenneth and Susie's 60th wedding anniversary party.

No matter how many times I went to the Dew Drop Inn, I never could take full inventory of everything in the store. Sometimes objects would catch my eye: an enormous glass Planters' Peanuts jar, a wooden toy tractor, stacks of greeting cards or the complete works of Alexander Dumas in red leather.

In a long, glass-enclosed case, salt and pepper shakers marked "Cookshire, Que.," pens and bulbous watches, all the remainders from travelling salesmen's wares, were arranged in permanent display. Many of the items were finally marked "Not for sale." Mr. Fraser, as I always called him, had become too attached to part with items that had never found a buyer.

In his musty, overflowing store-kingdom, Mr. Fraser was guardian of the small, forgotten stuff of life — trinkets taken for granted, fresh gumdrops and stories I could never hear often enough. On quiet, heavy afternoons, I would go to the Dew Drop Inn. I remember the creaking of the wooden stairs leading up to the door, the sound of the tinny bell ringing as I walked into the store, where ceiling-high shelves seemed to hold time at bay.

Buying a newspaper there was never a quick proposition, but rather an exchange requiring at least 10 minutes. The currency was good conversation over the worn wooden counter. "Now, did I tell you when ..." would start a tale of one of Cookshire's long-dead residents, that fella who fell into the horse water trough that used to be down at the corner, the other one who had tried to cheat at cards.

Mr. Fraser never forgot a name, a face, a mannerism of anyone he'd known, and as he evoked these characters, I was exhorted to reflect on the frailties of their human spirits. "O yes," he would say as an end to almost every story, "we didn't see that around here afterwards. He learned his lesson then."

Now, the Dew Drop Inn's long glass cabinet is in my husband's office, transparent and emptied. The store's entire merchandise is being sold in a seemingly endless garage sale. Mr. Fraser passed away before Christmas in his 89th year. I knew he had died just by the sight of the store, with snow piling up on the stairs, the light off inside. And there was no note tacked on the door, "Back in five minutes or hours."

Last week, it took all my courage to walk back into the store to see the sale and say hello. I bought a few boxes of greeting cards, a box of ancient soap, and a balsam-wood canoe paddle fancifully etched for tourists with "Cookshire, Que."

Last summer I was walking up the hill one evening, on the opposite side of the street from the store. The sunset illuminated the front porch where Mr. Fraser was sitting in the last amber light of the day. I kept turning around, as I walked, to look back at this timeless scene. Soon, places and people I've known will exist only in my mind.

Le Haut-Saint-François • 27 octobre 1994 • Page 27

COOKSHIRE
L'ancienne gare n'est plus

par Claude Leclerc

Le jeudi 29 septembre dernier, disparaissait un autre édifice du Canadien Pacific, celui de Cookshire situé à proximité de la meunerie Chapdeleine.

Avec lui, disparaissait également toute une époque, celle des chemins de fer du milieu du siècle. De fait, Cookshire fut sans contredit un point assez important dans le domaine ferroviaire de par sa situation géographique entre Montréal et Halifax, avec jonction vers la Nouvelle Angleterre.

Dominique Roy, retraité du CPR où il a passé la majorité de sa vie, relate que «durant les années 1940 à 1950, on pouvait dénombrer facilement une vingtaine de convois par jour, venant d'un peu partout.»

Plusieurs citoyens ont assisté au cours des années 1950 à la transformation des machines à vapeur pour celles à diesel. Aujourd'hui on est témoin d'une autre transformation, celle du train qui laisse la place aux camions lourds qui circulent sur nos routes parfois mal préparées pour ce genre de circulation. «Faut aller avec son temps, pour le meilleur et pour le pire», de préciser M. Roy.

C'est avec un sentiment partagé de nostalgie et de bon débarras que M. Dominique Roy regarde s'écrouler cette dernière partie de la gare CPR de Cookshire.

BROME COUNTY NEWS—Wednesday, November 2, 1994—7

Memories of Dew Drop Inn

It is hard to visualize Cookshire without the Dew Drop Inn. From 1929 until July 25 of this year, a simple sign welcoming visitors hung proudly on the front of what many of us now think of as an institution.

The building itself is over 125 years old and was constructed by Mr. Donahue of Sawyerville. Ken and Suzie Fraser purchased and started their restaurant and general store business in 1929.

Suzie said it was Ken who came up with the intriguing name for the business and many who knew him saw this as typical of his keen sense of humor and wit. The Dew Drop Inn was a restaurant, a general store, a gift shop and an inn for people travelling through town.

Besides running all these enterprises, Ken and Suzie provided meals at the Cookshire Fair for some 25 years. Ken was also a sign painter and painted beautiful signs for many of the businesses in the area including our own.

Seems Like Old Times
By Jean Murray Chute

LUCRATIVE
The restaurant part of the business was the most lucrative of the ventures, and was successful for many years until the war came and "our boys enlisted," as Suzie said.

Then times were difficult and Suzie decided she would have to do something to help make ends meet. She enrolled in the hairdressing school of Mrs. Campbell of East Angus and opened her own hair salon in the back of the store. She continued with her salon until the Parti Québécois took power in 1978 when they shut her salon down because she had not taken a French hairdressing course.

Being the feisty lady she was, she took a French course and passed, then continued serving the ladies of Cookshire and area.

As most people my age from the Cookshire area, I remember most going to the Dew Drop Inn for a snack after a school sports event. The place was never empty. You were usually greeted by Mr. and Mrs. Fraser and a handful of townsfolk gathered to talk over the events of the day or politics or whatever came up. It was a very welcoming place, consistent with its name.

After I married it became a place that I found myself in talking over the events of the day and taking in some of the Fraser's wisdom. It later became a place where my children visited for treats after school as I had so many years before.

HUGE TASK
Mr. Ken Fraser passed away last January and left his wife Suzie and their son Charles to start what seemed to be a colossal task — liquidating the contents of the store and house. They began by selling some of the large pieces of furniture, some of which I was very fortunate to get.

From then on, beginning in February until July 25, there was a continuous sale going on. Behind those beautiful antique counters and hidden in every nook and cranny of the building there were treasures to be found. We made many return trips and every time found something to buy. My final purchase was on the last day before Mrs. Frazer handed the keys over to the new owner. I purchased the old sign "Dew Drop Inn". Maybe it was sentiment that drove me, but there was always something so welcoming about that sign, that I felt compelled to find a place for it where it could again give that same feeling to others. It will get a fresh coat of paint and eventually welcome people to my antique shop.

The new owner, Mr. Alain Desaulnier, purchased the property to be demolished to make parking for his pharmacy next door. Mrs. Fraser has moved into a comfortable apartment just around the corner, still close to her friends and her memories.

Jean Murray Chute is owner of Classique Antiques in Lennoxville.

The Dew Drop Inn... the end of an institution.

Page 18 • *Le Haut-Saint-François* • 1er décembre 1994

COOKSHIRE
Le Dew Drop Inn n'est plus

La récente démolition du bâtiment Dew Drop Inn à Cookshire marque la disparition d'un vestige d'une autre époque. Cet établissement aux allures d'ancien magasin général avait un cachet particulier. Il suffisait de pénétrer à l'intérieur pour avoir l'impression de reculer dans le temps. L'atmosphère enveloppante nous permettait presque de sentir une époque aujourd'hui révolue. Aidé par la machinerie lourde, le bâtiment n'a mis que quelques minutes pour s'écrouler, comme s'il s'affaissait sous le poids des années.

65th straight fair for Cookshire veteran

By Claudia Villemaire

Her needle flies - down through the layers of material, back up - again and again, nimble fingers guiding its progress across an expanse of quilt top, leaving trails of tiny stitches that eventually become spirals or squares, binding together the latest of hundreds of quilts that this talented woman has created over more than six decades of sewing. Susie Fraser seemed quite at ease talking to this reporter by telephone this week even though she was working on a 'lap quilt' as we spoke. "I've been showing at Cookshire Fair for 65 years," she announces, affection for her hometown exhibition clear in her voice. "My son will be 64 this year and I showed for the first time a year before he was even born."

Susie's chuckling as she recalls her early days at the Frasers' Dew Drop Inn in Cookshire, where she operated a hairdressing parlour for nearly as many years, along with a gift shop at the back of the store.

She says she's never quite got over feeling sad about finally closing up shop. "My, I hated to leave my customers. That was very difficult, and then leaving my old home was worse. But there comes a time when you have to admit you need a bit of help with daily life." Brightening as we talk about her favourite pastime, Susie Fraser says she has "about 15 or so articles" going to the fair this year. "It takes me about a month to complete a quilt in a hurry, a bit longer if I take my time."

"I do regular block style, appliqué and plain everyday types of quilts, but you know there are lots of other things I like to sew too"

Susie is 93 and admits to slowing down a bit. "Of course, I don't have nearly as many things to take to the fair as I used to. This year I only have a couple pairs of socks, dresser scarves and table cloths and a few other things, besides a couple of quilts."

"That's much less than in those first years, when my husband would sometimes go to card parties five times a week. Well, I enjoyed staying home working on my quilts and we were both quite happy with that arrangement."

Sewing fanciers far and wide know about the Fraser quilts. Some have gone to the US, others across Canada. "I made three quilts, exactly the same, for a man who wanted to give his daughters a special gift."

"Then there's the quilt a bridegroom ordered for his bride but forgot to tell me about the order until one month before the wedding. By the time we had the materials, specifically all blue, I had less than a month to complete the task. I got it done but had to burn the midnight oil quite a bit."

Will Mrs. Fraser drop in at Cookshire Fair herself? "Oh yes, I'll try to get to the fair to visit with all my friends. But I think those stairs would do me in so I won't be able to get upstairs to see all the arts and crafts. But, at my age, I suppose I should be thankful to be there."

She still works needlepoint and cross-stitch patterns and still gets out to visit family in the Cookshire area.

"My eyes are good and so is my health," she laughs. "I spent five weeks with my nephew Mac Fraser this summer and I do enjoy getting back to the country," she says.

Of course, she brought her sewing work with her. "No time to stop that - and besides, I wouldn't know what to do with myself without some sewing in my hands."

www.ingramcontent.com/pod-product-compliance
Lightning Source LLC
Chambersburg PA
CBHW070600010526
44118CB00012B/1394